How to Assess and Measure Business Innovation

How to Assess and Measure Business Innovation

Magnus Penker, Peter Junermark, and Sten Jacobson

ISBN-13: 9781535160988
ISBN-10: 1535160985
Library of Congress Control Number: 2017909759
CreateSpace Independent Publishing Platform
North Charleston, South Carolina

CONTENTS

FOREWORD

In business, there has to be a healthy balance between innovation and short-term results. Yet too many organizations still lean toward the latter. This book series will convince you that this tendency is bad for value, profit, and progress alike.

I am the CEO of CellMark, a company moving products and services worth US$3 billion per year, with sixty-five offices in thirty countries. Despite our success so far, we are currently transforming ourselves from a traditional trader to an "instant international" network for entrepreneurs—innovating a stagnant business model by enabling entrepreneurs to innovate more freely and globally. In CellMark, I see very real parallels in our experiences and the insights within these pages. Mr. Penker and his Innovation360 colleagues provide the fact-based tools and forward-looking approach today's businesses need to become innovation driven without compromising short-term results.

I like to think of the CellMark structure around innovation as making sure that we don't do our fishing in the parking lot—instead, we go where the fish are. As an entrepreneurial leader, driving value through innovation has become my passion. This book series and its step-by-step process for creating short-, mid-, and long-term value through innovation just might do the same for you.

—Fredrik Andersson, June 20, 2017

ACKNOWLEDGMENTS

There are so many people who deserve credit and thanks for this work that I could fill several more volumes with names alone. Ideas come into the world on their own schedule, often to many people at once who are oceans apart and working in disconnected fields. I want to personally thank everyone who shared in the formation of the ideas presented here, and I hope to live long enough to say so to each of you in person.

For now, I would like to recognize a few of the individuals who did extraordinary work to encapsulate these concepts in their present form.

First of all, my thanks go out to the faculty, staff, and students at the Henley Business School in the United Kingdom, where the Innovation360 project took its first breath of inspiration. In particular, I want to express my gratitude to George Tovstiga, Henley's Distinguished Professor of Strategy and Innovation, whose support and encouragement at the earliest stages of my research project truly set the foundation for Innovation360 and the work presented in this series of volumes.

The entire team at Innovation360 knows they have my profound thanks and respect for helping bring new ideas into the world. That also includes those outside the company who have made valuable contributions, such as Dragan Bilic and Henrik Lundblad for their graphical work, and Sasha Viasasha and Annginette Anderson for their editorial help. I'd also like to thank all our clients and all independent Innovation360 licensed practitioners who are working in the field right now to support the next generation of innovators. I would especially like to mention Niclas Claesson, Julia Doria, Anders Bjurstam, Marcus Wahlberg, Martin Hultqvist, Paulo Malta, Agnes Sävenstedt, Tomas Wolf, Jens Nilsson, Lars-Göran Fröjd, Peet van Biljon, Sabina Svensson, Allan Ashok, Saif Amer, Nahid Mammadov, Thierry Bernicard, Laura Duran, and Peter Glasheen for their profound contributions.

Finally, I want to thank my coauthors on this volume, Sten Jacobson and Peter Junermark. I am thrilled to share these pages with them and their brilliant insights.

CHAPTER 1

THE COMPLETE GUIDE TO BUSINESS INNOVATION, VOLUMES 1 TO 5

The past can no longer be a predictor. The forces reshaping global culture have become so sweeping and multifaceted that a company's past successes have lost their statistical weight in projections of what is most likely to happen next.

There have been only a few other historical precedents of times like the one we are in now, and the postchange world looks absolutely nothing like the world before.

The World's Four Revolutions

We are now living in the midst of the Fourth Industrial Revolution, fundamentally rewriting the rules of how we live, work, and relate to one another. Somewhere in the world right now, there is most probably a working prototype of an innovation that will be as profound as the Internet or self-aware AI.

The World Economic Forum introduced this conceptual framework for global development in 2016, but the evidence has been right in front of us for a great deal longer.

The First Industrial Revolution in the eighteenth century transformed the world of work from animal-powered labor to mechanical drivers. The Second in the nineteenth century brought to bear electricity and previously unimagined economies of scale. The Third in the twentieth century transferred industrial logistical control to computers and automation.

Now, in the twenty-first century, we are witnessing the convergence of all past advances in power and energy. Mechanical devices, electricity, and networked computers are merging with biological systems. Honestly, no one has any idea where that will lead us.

The Path Ahead

In its scale, scope, and complexity, our revolution is ushering in a world unlike anything we have experienced. Like the world of quantum mechanics, common sense does not apply to uncommon environments. While we cannot know how this will unfold on the macro level, each organization can take control of its own innovation strategy.

In order for their organization to play a consequential role in the sweeping changes swirling all around it and to benefit from them, leaders must follow a praxis that is integrated and comprehensive, involving all external and internal stakeholders.

If there are any omissions or vulnerabilities in the foundations of their business strategy, market forces will simply tear it apart. Successful leaders adhere to a methodology that aligns strategy, leadership styles, internal culture, untapped capabilities, and adaptable competencies.

A Comprehensive Innovation Strategy

Solid research indicates that a coordinated innovation strategy has been and will be the key to success in building innovative, sustainable business models that thrive amid the turbulent times ahead. Organizations that aspire to persistent relevancy need a true, reliable, and easily measurable 360-degree understanding of what just happened, what is happening at the moment, and which potential futures are most likely to occur.

Entrepreneur and international innovation expert Magnus Penker built the Innovation360 Group to offer businesses a pathway for achieving that understanding. Penker's journey began with a deceptively simple question: "Why do some innovative firms change the world while others struggle to survive?" In analyzing data from thousands of businesses, Penker concluded that it's not a matter of luck, although timing matters. It's not just talent, a well-connected board, or intelligent funding choices.

The Value of the InnoSurvey

The answer can seem stultifyingly elusive, but the underlying truth is that each organization contains its own individual seeds of success or failure. Repeatable success depends on leaders nurturing the right combination of elements with exquisite precision.

Penker and his team studied more than a thousand companies across sixty-two countries to build the world's largest innovation database, the InnoSurvey. This contains a compilation of insights from multiple respondents in each company (both external and internal stakeholders) that arrives at a comprehensive 360-degree analysis of what, why, and how innovation projects came to fruition.

Over the years, the team has been able to refine and develop these specialized methods for anatomizing innovation. This approach provides an iterative, evidence-based assessment to serve as the road map for future investments.

The Overarching Goal

The goal of this book series is to help more great ideas find practical expression and help more companies survive despite market upheavals.

The five volumes cover:

Part One: How to Assess and Measure Business Innovation
Part Two: The Elements of Innovation
Part Three: A Complete Innovation System from Ideation to Governance
Part Four: Tactical Innovation Techniques in Practice
Part Five: Sustainable Growth and Profits from Managing Your Innovation Strategy, Organization, and Portfolio

While things are changing with blinding speed and large-scale cultural shifts are resetting the market's priorities in unpredictable ways, there's no reason to throw up your hands. This book is meant to be a firm grounding you can return to again and again. There are many precedents within the InnoSurvey to help you make sense of what's happening with each innovation you introduce.

What the world has in store for the years ahead is very likely to be radically, shockingly new, but you can prepare yourself and your organization to soar above the whirlwind. As you work your way through this series, you will nail down a repeatable, teachable process to innovate for greater profits and market share—no matter how the world changes.

CHAPTER 2

INTRODUCTION TO *HOW TO ASSESS AND MEASURE BUSINESS INNOVATION*

There have been many brilliant innovations in history that went nowhere.

Many brought fame and fortune to later adopters of these ideas, some who lived much later and are now credited with introducing these innovations to the world. This distinguished list of ideas whose time had not yet come could include movable-type printing. Inaccurately attributed to Gutenberg in 1440, this was actually invented in 1041 by Chinese polymath Bi Sheng. Arguably, you could also include computer programming, which had its central logic laid out by Ada Lovelace in 1843, a century before there were any computers to program. Undoubtedly, there is a great deal that could and should be salvaged from the world's current list of neglected innovations.

Innovation Lost

A more relevant and recent example might be LoudCloud. Marc Andreessen, one of the most successful entrepreneurs and venture capitalists in the world, launched this cloud-computing provider with $120 million in seed funding and an open market of $5.9 billion. You probably haven't heard of it; it doesn't exist anymore. LoudCloud was broken up and sold off in pieces. You can't really call the innovation a failure, because its technology is still generating revenue, but that revenue is flowing to other companies.

What went wrong? A proper analysis could fill a book by itself, but part of the answer is that the world wasn't ready yet. LoudCloud entered the market in 1999, a decade before Software-as-a-Service (SaaS) computing and storage went mainstream.

To successfully navigate the forces of change and disruption, the leaders of today's organizations are tasked with one major challenge, namely reliable growth in an uncertain market landscape. Given current conditions and outlooks, the greatest risk you could take is to do nothing.

The Odds of Survival

According to some leading market estimates, four out of ten businesses that dominate their verticals today won't even exist within a decade, and the ones that do survive will be transformed by technologies still in their infancy today.

Barriers to entry have never been so low, and product and company life cycles have never been so short. Simple optimization of current resources, processes, and business models is not enough. The central question each leader needs to answer is, "Where do we grow next?" Taking a chance is an unacceptable risk when so much is at stake. You will need a more insightful, data-driven way to define your investment in innovation—and that path begins here.

By its very nature, innovation seeks to challenge the status quo by making better, unique products and services using existing resources, capabilities, and competences in new ways. The goal is to satisfy unmet needs, whatever they may be, by using and/or developing technology to make the impossible possible. Innovation can be done in small steps (incremental) or in leaps (radical). Everything external as well as internal can be innovated. Some innovations are designed to impact profit, while others are meant to grow market share, but each innovation affects the others within an organization's Wheel of Innovation™. However, pursuing different innovations requires the adoption of equally different perceptions, mind-sets, and goal-setting approaches. Thus, innovators and innovation managers need to be active in different "time horizons" at the same time.

Working with Three Innovation Horizons

The Innovation360 approach is inspired by Steve Coley's work that defined how innovation can be divided into three parallel horizons. Each evolves along a predictable S curve.

The first horizon (H1) concerns smaller, incremental innovations that build on existing business models, extending the existing S curve of the company. These can normally be accomplished with little structural change and lead time. The second horizon (H2) is more creative and proactive, expanding and building new businesses into new directions.

The third horizon (H3) is sometimes characterized as "moon shots" or "skunk works." This is a much more explorative approach to future S curves, to be commercialized in H2, ending up producing significant cash flows in H1. Ideally, a company should be working on all three horizons simultaneously.

The biggest failure of many contemporary strategies is that they are stuck in H1. Some studies indicate that up to 99 percent of businesses are trapped there due to "spiral staircase" leadership. In the interest of safety and risk aversion, leaders mandate step-by-step projects with narrowly defined goals and predictable ROI. This strategy has also been compared to arranging deck chairs on the *Titanic*, a futile action in the face of an impending catastrophe.

When this happens, large H1 projects tend to get prioritized to the extent that they generate internal traffic jams among projects that must share resources. The result is too many, too big, and too cautious projects that don't create value for the firm or their customers.

The Roles of Assessment and Measurement

A more successful approach has been seen in companies that deploy limited resources more optimally, nurturing today's profit (H1), developing new ideas for tomorrow's profit and market share (H2), and taking part in building the future (H3).

To link strategic direction and business modeling in a hypercompetitive market with change and transformation programs for driving successful business development in several horizons, one must have a thorough comprehension of what "innovation management" means within the context of your own organization. Turning the principles of successful innovation into something that can be assessed and measured will be the subject of this book, part one in a series that will take you from quantification to execution of your innovation strategy. In particular, the assessment and measurement of the organization's innovation capabilities both deserve a prominent place on the agenda of all C-levels, entrepreneurs, business owners, venture capitalists, and practitioners working with business development/R and D.

Optimizing Innovation Investments

By using the framework in this book, you can use your findings to establish the most effective strategy, leadership, culture, capabilities, and competences needed to drive optimal innovation in the first, second, and third horizons, mitigating risk in a changing market landscape and identifying the smartest moves for short-, mid-, and long-term profitability.

In the pages ahead, you will be introduced to *innovation analytics*. More than just a theoretical construct, innovation analytics is a praxis for turning the possible into the real. As you apply innovation analytics to your own organization, you will learn how to interpolate data on the competitive landscape and the dynamics of how the market will react to the introduction of your innovative ideas. You will develop an understanding of how to quantify all major drivers—industrial as well as macro key—in the bigger picture. You will oversee a comprehensive investigation of the organization's business capabilities that we call the *360-degree analysis*. This analysis is a living document that will grow and evolve in tandem with internal and external changes from technology drivers.

Common creative solutions, crowdsourcing, social media, online intermediaries, and Massive Open Online Courses (MOOC) are just a few of the underlying driving technologies that are fundamentally changing the landscape, opening a window of opportunity to firms with innovative capabilities to service and drive these new markets. These capabilities include multistrategy capabilities, the use of in-depth consumer insights, an agile organization, advanced networking and linkages, platform thinking, and technology watch.

The end result will be a compendium of tangible data that can be used to model or remodel the business structure, the overall strategy, and the related transformation projects that will set the staging area for your innovation's best possible launch.

Let's make it happen.

CHAPTER 3

AN INTRODUCTION TO CURRENT THINKING ON INNOVATION

Innovation is commonly defined as the introduction of new technologies (*Encyclopedia Britannica* 1974), and is held by some writers to be a primary factor in economic growth. This notion forms the core of the interpretation used in this volume. Innovations are driven by opportunities and capabilities. In particular, Drucker (1998) identified four areas of opportunity where innovation possibilities occur: unexpected occurrences, contradictions, process needs, and industry and market changes.

There are three additional sources of opportunity external to a given company: demographic changes, changes in perception, and new knowledge. It is also possible to consider linkage to another organization or organizations as an asset in itself. Tovstiga and Birchall (2005) argue that firms are nodes in larger networks that create value by transforming opportunities into business through the strategic deployment of capabilities. Moreover, they argue that firms are constantly looking for opportunities within the environment to turn a competitive advantage through transformation innovation, ultimately gaining profitable growth. To summarize, innovation can be seen from two perspectives: from the internal perspective of a firm's capabilities and from the external-market perspective, where performance can be measured and success judged (Tovstiga and Birchall 2005).

Depending on the kind of innovation strategy they adopt, companies and organizations can be categorized into three types: need seekers, market readers, and technology drivers. *Need seekers* look for potential opportunities by applying superior understanding of the market and rapid go-to-market initiatives; *market readers* capitalize on existing trends and understanding of markets; and *technology drivers* strive for breakthrough innovations based on new technology (Jaruzelski and Dehoff 2010). Recent research based on more than ten years of measurement shows that need-seeking organizations that have aligned their strategies with their capabilities are the most successful in generating return on investment in R and D (Jaruzelski, Staack, and Goehle 2014).

In current thinking, there are several types of innovations, including what is called *strategic innovation* and *innovation of business models*. In another trend, known as *open innovation*, innovations are driven in symbiosis with external parties. Many practitioners and academics emphasize the importance of building the right capabilities and adopting the right leadership style, as well as understanding and developing corporate culture in a way that maximizes the value of innovation work. In this section, we review each of these systems and approaches to innovation in some detail.

3.1 Scope and Types of Innovation

Innovation can be categorized by four levels of aggregation. In the first, there are improvements on an individual level; the second (functional) level includes changes to processes; the third (company level) typically concerns the value chain and radical product and service innovations; and the fourth (industry) level typically concerns breakthrough innovations that change the playing field. Another way of categorizing innovation is based on whether it is aiming at a new market or not, as well as its level of aggregation or scope; these two dimensions can be combined, as illustrated in figure 1.

The nature of innovations can be described by their scope in combination with either a quantifiable or nonquantifiable outcome (Tovstiga and Birchall 2005). Tovstiga and Birchall (2005) and Assink (2006) identify scope or aggregation level as one of the two characteristics and the market or the outcome as the other.

Tovstiga and Birchall (2005) consider quantifiable and operational scope as institutional innovations, while Assink (2006) classifies technology, concept, or product innovations with existing means in an existing market as incremental innovations. Moreover, Tovstiga and Birchall (2005) call nonquantifiable and strategic scope "radical innovations," while Assink (2006) describes new technology, concept, or product innovations in a new existing market as "breakthrough innovations" (see figure 1). In this text, we will use these terms interchangeably.

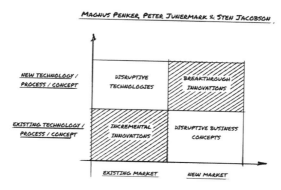

Figure 1: Innovation Framework (Source: Assink 2006).

In the international best seller *Blue Ocean Strategy*, Kim and Mauborgne (1997, 2005) argue that the conventional approach to staying ahead of competitors is less successful than making the competitors irrelevant by applying what they call "value innovation," the cornerstone of their "blue ocean strategy" concept. They define conventional logic as a "red ocean" where companies apply current industry logic to the tasks of gaining competitive advantage and both keeping existing customers and expanding the customer base through linear expansion. In contrast to the red ocean, companies that use a blue-ocean strategy make the competition irrelevant by innovating new, uncontested market spaces where they can operate successfully. This is one example of a how radical innovation can be applied.

In blue-ocean strategy, there are three platforms for innovating by applying value innovation: product, service, and delivery platforms.

According to Kim and Mauborgne (2015), when applying the blue-ocean strategy based on value innovation, there are eight principles to follow such as the following:

Formulation Principles:

- Reconstruct market boundaries.
- Focus on the big picture, not the numbers.
- Reach beyond existing demand.
- Get the strategic sequence right.

Execution Principles:

- Overcome key organizational hurdles.
- Build execution into strategy.
- Align the value, profit, and people propositions.
- Renew blue oceans.

Traditionally, innovation has often been tightly associated with design. Over the years, design-centric principles have expanded from solely product innovation to also being applied to strategy. *Design thinking* aims to create significant change rather than incremental improvements, making it an efficient tool for achieving radical innovation. The notion of seeing the way designers think and act as a process or methodology was first introduced in the seventies (Simon 1969; McKim 1973). During the nineties, it was applied to business development and strategy and popularized by David M. Kelley and Tim Brown of IDEO and Roger Martin of the Rotman School (Brown and Martin 2015).

Design thinking is a strategy-making process divided into three major stages. The first phase aims to invent a future from a customer point of view. Customers are observed to formulate hypotheses focusing on what they might want in the invented future but don't have today. In the second phase, those hypotheses are tested through iterative prototyping and adjusted based on user reactions. The third phase brings the ideas, products, or services to life by making sure you have the capabilities in place to produce, distribute, and sell the product or service (Brown and Martin 2015).

Eric Ries (2011) emphasizes the importance of speeding up the learning cycles of the iterative prototyping process while continuously collecting data. Ries (2011) suggests the development of a Minimum Viable Product (MVP) that is tested with a first paying customer in iterations of build, measure, and learn. Ries terms those iterations *validated learning cycles*.

Both *design thinking* and *lean startup* champion a user-centric approach with a tolerance for mistakes, focusing on need-seeker strategy to identify and resolve the customer job-to-be-done.

By definition, *revenue growth* comes from selling more products and services to more customers or from selling more valuable (i.e., higher-price) products and services—or both. Geographical expansion and acquisition activity also enable revenue growth. Innovation drives increased value in the eyes of your customers, allowing a higher price point. It also helps you adapt to the challenges of pursuing new markets, whether in different geographical, demographic, or industry segments. Market-share increases can be enabled by superior innovation (often radical innovation) or by commercial means such as aggressive sales or pricing tactics (often linked to incremental innovation with new features or reduced production cost). However, in the long run—due to the cycle of "creative destruction" that occurs in all industries—maintaining and growing revenue ultimately depends on refreshing and expanding your current range of products and services.

Except for the dimensions of scope and market innovation, all the characteristics discussed so far might be categorized within a typology defined and illustrated by Trott (2008), shown in table 1. The type of innovation gives us a common language to characterize, compare, and contrast different kinds of possible innovation, regardless of whether they are incremental or radical.

Type of Innovation	Example
Product Innovation	The development of a new or improved product.
Process Innovation	The development of a new manufacturing process.
Organizational Innovation	A new venture division; a new internal communication system; introduction of a new accounting procedure.
Management Innovation	TQM (total quality management) systems; BPR (business processes reengineering).
Production Innovation	Quality circles; just-in-time (JIT) manufacturing systems; new production-planning software.
Commercial/Marketing Innovation	New financing arrangements; new sales; delivery innovations in sales; or market approaches, e.g., direct marketing). This is also referred to as *business model innovation,* meaning the development of new or improved business models and value propositions.
Service Innovation	Internet-based financial services.

Table 1: Typology of innovations adopted with explanations and examples (Source: Trott 2008).

Understanding the scope, approach, and typology of innovations builds an understanding of both the need for innovation capabilities of an organization and how to use them in the optimal way.

3.2 Strategic Innovations

Strategic moves, as described by Kim and Mauborgne (2015), are managerial actions and decisions that fundamentally change the business, open new markets, and result in large leaps in demand. Moreover, Kim and Mauborgne (2015) argue that strategic moves offer an organization the possibility of profitable growth instead of the prospect of becoming stuck in the red ocean, as described earlier in this section.

Govindarajan and Trimble (2005) point out that strategic innovations and entrepreneurship are imperative to success in a globalized world, where the economic environment is rapidly changing. Moreover, it is in the process of strategic innovations that new potential customers are explored, delivery of value is conceptualized and analyzed, and the end-to-end value chain is explored and redesigned.

Strategic innovations are like experiments, with several key characteristics: they obtain leverage on an organization's existing capabilities but are not line extensions; they are launched ahead of competitors; they require at least some new capability and knowledge; they are unprofitable during the first period of time; and it is initially hard to judge whether they are successful or not. Strategic innovations are driven as projects and use the existing business as a platform.

In contrast, *management innovations* are about changing the platform and the core principle of the business. A management innovation creates long-lasting advantage when it meets one or more of three conditions: the innovation is based on a novel principle that challenges management orthodoxy; it is systemic, encompassing a range of processes and methods; and it is a part of an ongoing program of invention, where progress compounds over time (Hamel 2006, 74).

Management innovation is about management-process innovation, while another innovation is about business processes, such as the supply chain and customer support. Managerial work typically focuses on setting goals, coordinating the use of resources and activities, acquiring knowledge, identifying and developing talents, and building and nurturing relationships. According to Hamel (2006), the elements of management innovation are the following:

- Commitment to a big management problem
- Novel principles that illuminate new approaches
- Deconstruction of management orthodoxies
- Analogies from atypical organizations that redefine what's possible

A business model "consists of four interlocking elements that, taken together, create and deliver value" (Johnson, Christensen, and Kagermann 2008, 52), and is one of several possible areas for management innovation. According to Teece (2010), new-product development should be complemented by a new business model that defines the go-to-market and value-capture strategies.

Teece (2010) points out two extremes of business models: an integrated business model at one extreme and an outsourced business model at the other. In the integrated business model, all activities—from design and manufacturing to sales and distribution—are done in-house. In the outsourced model, the business focuses on core capabilities and outsources the rest; one extreme example is Dolby, which offers high-fidelity noise reduction through a pure licensing model where everything is outsourced.

In practice, new business models often do not generate new growth because management does not fully understand the current business model and thus has difficulty judging whether to use the current business model or to reinvent it. Any business model, new or established, comprises three elements: a profit formula, key resources, and key processes (Johnson, Christensen, and Kagermann 2008). The first, the *profit formula*, is a combination of a revenue model, cost structure, a margin model, and resource velocity, which refers to inventory turnover and other aspects of resource utilization. *Key resources* are what's needed to operate, while *key processes* concern *how* to operate and measure results.

3.3 The Business-Model Generation and Value-Proposition Design

An emerging de facto standard for business-model generation and value-proposition design are the two "canvases" proposed by Osterwalder and Pigneur (2010). These canvases, which are tightly connected to each other, provide a visual modeling standard for innovating new business models and/or value propositions. They provide a structured approach to working with value innovation, starting in the ideation phase as a brainstorming/workshop tool and leading all the way to strategic-development projects and implementation. The techniques used in this approach support all types of innovation; integrate smoothly with other conceptual models such as the blue ocean strategy; and have a strong focus on in-depth understanding of customer anthropology—that is, "gains," "pains," and "jobs to get done." Hence, the relatively new role of the "business anthropologist" is becoming crucial to understanding your customers, increasing your innovation capability, and designing and implementing new blue-ocean strategies.

3.4 Open Innovation

Open-market innovation refers to the free trade of innovations among external parties within the innovation process. Innovation exchange, innovation databases, access to venture capital, and innovation agents are driving open-market innovation and can yield positive impacts on an organization, providing insights into what the core business actually is, improving employee retention, and potentially increasing revenues through licensing fees (Rigby and Zook 2002).

Henry Chesbrough, a well-known champion of open innovation, argues that open innovation can be seen as "outside-in" (where a company uses external ideas in its business) or "inside-out" (where companies offer open platforms and technologies to the market).

Examples of the inside-out model are Amazon, where internal web-based systems are offered to customers that drive Amazon revenue, and the LEGO Group, which allowed external parties to develop their new concept of programmable toy robots (MINDSTORMS®). The key to competitive advantage in open innovation is to understand the service value web, where the company and the market interact to create value (Chesbrough 2011). In another more recent move, LEGO became seriously involved in the market for business modeling and business-model innovations by launching their new LEGO kit, LEGO SeriousPlay®. LEGO SeriousPlay lends itself to business modeling in general but also directly to specific approaches to business modeling, such as the two canvases of Osterwalder and Pigneur (2010).

Figure 2 shows Chesbrough's (2011) reconceptualization of Michael Porter's value chain. Chesbrough argues that the focus should be on what creates primary value, and thus, his new *service value web* addresses the weak point in Porter's value chain: customer interaction.

Huston and Sakkab (2006) point out that sharing innovations with external parties (or "networks") does not guarantee revenue. Rather, these systems can, depending on how they are used, connect ideas and capabilities, as in, for example, Procter and Gamble's innovation model, Connect and Develop.

On the other hand, Nambisan and Sawhney (2007) argue that ideas and/or market-ready concepts can be easily bought; a kind of outsourcing in itself. When shopping for ideas or market-ready concepts, however, management needs to take both industry factors and company factors into consideration. Industry factors that typically need to be considered are the pace of technological and market change, innovation potential, and costs.

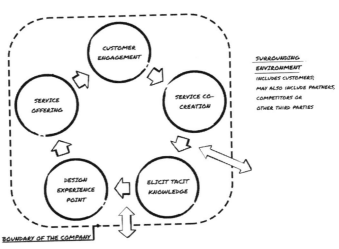

Figure 2: Service value web (Source: Chesbrough 2011).

Typically, the company factors to be considered are the purpose of the innovation, product capabilities, company size, and the company's appetite for risk. One example of outside innovations where external parties drive innovation is the hardware game-console manufacturer Nintendo, which encourages third-party businesses to develop and sell games on their platform (Boudreau and Lakhani 2009).

Boudreau and Lakhani identified three critical issues that managers should take into account when they decide to engage in open innovation: (1) the type of innovation, (2) the motivation of the individual innovating, and (3) the nature of the platform business model (Boudreau and Lakhani 2009, 70).

Boudreau and Lakhani also characterize the motivations of external innovators as either *extrinsic* or *intrinsic*, where *open markets* (e.g., iTunes) are driven by extrinsic motivations such as money and the need for development, while *communities* (e.g., Linux) are driven by intrinsic motivations such as identity, fun, and intellectual challenges.

There are three kinds of platforms for innovation: integrator platforms, product platforms, and two-sided platforms. *Integrator platforms* are platforms (e.g., iTunes and iPhone) where customers connect with innovators through the platform, while *product platforms* (e.g., Gore-Tex) offer external innovators the potential for both innovating and selling to customers; the two-sided platform is typically an affiliate program where external innovators interact directly with customers.

However, there are issues such as intellectual-property rights that could cause companies difficulties using the results of innovation when people outside the organization have generated ideas (Brinkinshaw, Bouquet, and Barsoux 2011).

3.5 Leadership and Culture

Culture and leadership are key to innovation management and creativity, especially when it comes to composition of teams and leadership styles. As an interesting example, Rigby, Gruver, and Allen (2009) argue that creative fashion businesses are virtually always led by a right-brained individual with imagination, in partnership with a left-brained individual with analytical skills. Another possibility of getting the right dynamic is to "assemble small incubation teams to help directors refine their own ideas" (Catmull 2008). According to Leonard and Straus (1997), the mix of the teams is important, and "if you want an innovative organization, you need to hire, work with, and promote people who make you uncomfortable...you need to understand your own preferences so that you can complement your weaknesses and exploit your strengths" (Leonard and Straus 1997).

According to Kelly and Littman (2005), there are ten personas typically needed to drive creativity through an organization. "The Devil's Advocate may never go away, but on a good day, the ten personas can keep him in place" (Kelly and Littman 2005). The idea is to create a climate and culture that stimulate innovation, from idea to results. One person might provide the team with one or several personas; the important thing is to make sure all profiles are present within an organization to stimulate and support innovation processes.

Kelly and Littman divide the ten personas into three categories: learning personas, organizational personas, and building personas.

3.5.1 Learning Personas

The *learning personas* are individuals digging for new sources and knowledge.

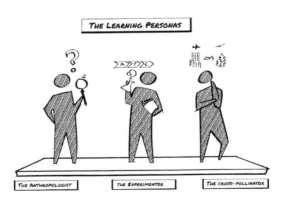

THE LEARNING PERSONAS

THE ANTHROPOLOGIST | THE EXPERIMENTER | THE CROSS-POLLINATOR

3.5.1.1 Persona: the Anthropologist

The *anthropologist* is rarely stationary. Rather, this is the person who ventures into the field to observe how people interact with products, services, and experiences, in order to come up with new innovations. The anthropologist is extremely good at reframing a problem in a new way and humanizing scientific method to apply it to daily life. Anthropologists share such distinguishing characteristics as the wisdom to observe with a truly open mind, empathy, intuition, the ability to see things that have gone unnoticed, a tendency to keep running lists of innovative concepts worth emulating and problems that need solving, and a habit of seeking inspiration in unusual places.

3.5.1.2 Persona: Cross-Pollinator

The *cross-pollinator* draws associations and connections between seemingly unrelated ideas or concepts to break new ground. Armed with a wide set of interests, an avid curiosity, and an aptitude for learning and teaching, the cross-pollinator brings big ideas in from the outside world to enliven the organization. People in this role can often be identified by their open-mindedness, diligent note-taking, tendency to think in metaphors, and ability to reap inspiration from the constraints persona.

3.5.1.3 Persona: Experimenter

The *experimenter* celebrates the process, not the tools, testing, and re-testing potential scenarios needed to make ideas tangible. A calculated risk-taker, this person models everything from products to services and proposals in order to reach solutions efficiently. To share the fun of discovery, the experimenter invites others to collaborate, all the while making sure the entire process is saving time and money.

3.5.2 Organizational Personas

Organizational personas are the ones structuring, challenging, and orchestrating the work.

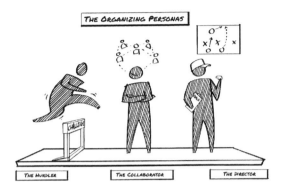

3.5.1.1 Persona: Hurdler

The *hurdler* is a tireless problem-solver who gets a charge out of tackling things that have never been done before. When confronted with a challenge, the hurdler gracefully sidesteps the obstacle while maintaining a quiet, positive determination. This optimism and perseverance can help upend the status quo with implementable big ideas as well as turning setbacks into the organization's greatest successes—despite doomsday forecasting by shortsighted experts.

3.5.1.2 Persona: Director

The *director* has an acute understanding of the bigger picture and a firm grasp on the pulse of the organization. Consequently, the director is talented at setting the stage, targeting opportunities, bringing out the best in their players, and getting things done. Through empowerment and inspiration, people in this role motivate those around them to take center stage and embrace the unexpected.

3.5.1.3 Persona: Collaborator

The *collaborator* is the rare person who truly values the team over the individual. In the interest of getting things done, the collaborator coaxes people out of their work silos to form multidisciplinary teams. In doing so, the person in this role dissolves traditional boundaries within organizations and creates opportunities for team members to assume new roles. More of a coach than a boss, the collaborator instills teams with the confidence and skills needed to reach the shared objective.

3.5.3 Building Personas

Building personas are typically the intellectual architects, the storytellers, and the caregivers as well as the ones setting up a proper environment.

3.5.3.1 Persona: Experience Architect

The *experience architect* is a person who relentlessly focuses on creating remarkable individual experiences. This person facilitates positive encounters with his or her organization through products, services, digital interactions, spaces, or events. Whether an engineer or a sushi chef, the experience architect maps out how to turn something ordinary into something distinctive.

3.5.3.2 Persona: Set Designer

The *set designer* views every day as a chance to liven up his or her workspace. These people promote energetic, inspired cultures by creating work environments that celebrate the individual and stimulate creativity. To keep up with shifting needs and foster continuous innovation, the set designer makes adjustments to a physical space to balance private and collaborative work opportunities. In doing so, this person makes space itself one of the organization's most versatile and powerful tools.

3.5.3.3 Persona: Storyteller

The *storyteller* captures our imagination with compelling narratives of initiative, hard work, and innovation. This person goes beyond oral tradition to work in whatever medium best fits his or her skills and message: video, narrative, animation, or even comic strips. By rooting these stories in authenticity, the storyteller can spark emotion and action, transmit values and objectives, foster collaboration, create heroes, and lead people and organizations into the future.

3.5.3.4 Persona: Caregiver

The *caregiver* is the foundation of human-powered innovation. Through empathy, caregivers work to understand each individual customer and to create a relationship. Whether a nurse in a hospital, a salesperson in a retail shop, or a teller at an international financial institution, the caregiver guides clients through the process to provide them a comfortable, human-centered experience.

3.5.4 Leadership and Breakthroughs

People, team composition, and leadership are all important components in the process of running the creative work. However, the management team needs an additional skill to guide and orchestrate the brainstorming process and ask the right questions, so that their people make actionable breakthroughs when brainstorming.

Generally speaking, people are not very efficient at running unstructured and abstract discussions without clear goals, or slicing data in all kinds of ways. Instead, exploring unexpected success, looking at other trades with similar challenges and boundaries, and examining binding constraints are more effective ways of orchestrating the creative processes (Coyne, Clifford, and Dye 2007).

Moreover, people need to be motivated and encouraged. As discussed previously, motivation may be both intrinsic and extrinsic. In this context, extrinsic motivation alone is not enough: if not complemented with intrinsic motivation, it can actually destroy creativity, as people can feel controlled or manipulated. Intrinsic motivation is the stronger of the two, because it gives people's work meaning. It can be fostered by assigning appropriate tasks to the most suitable people, giving them freedom, allocating sufficient resources, and encouraging work (Amabile 1998).

A well-known innovative practitioner, Steve Jobs, has developed seven principles for breakthrough thinking and success, which are the following:

Principle 1: Do What You Love
Principle 2: Put a Dent in the Universe
Principle 3: Kick-Start Your Brain
Principle 4: Sell Dreams, Not Products
Principle 5: Say No to 1,000 Things
Principle 6: Create Insanely Great Experience
Principle 7: Master the Message

(Source: Gallo 2011)

3.5.5 Classification of Leadership Styles for Innovation

A key part of the leadership challenge in an innovating organization is that different kinds of innovation problems call for different kinds of leadership (Loewe, Williamson, and Wood 2001). Loewe, Williamson, and Wood identify five leadership styles that can be combined and used to cover the range from incremental to radical innovation that are the following:

Leadership	Definition
The Cauldron	An entrepreneurial style where the business model is frequently challenged.
The Spiral Staircase	A style where you climb upward without losing the overall goal.
The Fertile Field	A style where the organization tries to use existing capabilities and resources in a new way.
The Pac-Man	A style where you invent, outsource, and finance startups.
The Explorer	A style where you explore possibilities and invest time and money in them without demanding short-term profit.

Table 2. Five kinds of leadership (Source: Loewe, Williamson, and Wood 2001).

3.5.6 Spinoffs and Ventures

Govindarajan and Trimble (2005) have pointed out the importance of letting strategic innovations become new ventures that borrow resources from the corporation (mother company) but are not influenced by past success or cultural principles, like commonly accepted dos and don'ts.

Ventures may be spinoffs, strategic experiments, or innovations in business models, but all are strategic innovations driven as separate ventures founded, financed, and deployed with the corporation's resources (staff, systems, structures, and/or culture) that are autonomous and eventually led by externally hired management (Govindarajan and Trimble 2005).

According to Day (2007), innovations can be structured and managed within a portfolio in order to handle risk and revenue. "By managing potential revenue and risk within a portfolio of innovation projects, better return can be reached over time."

The current literature on the topic of innovation cites a combination of factors that are fundamental to success: leadership, culture, how teams are put together, risk and portfolio management of the innovation process, and potential and controlled spinoff of strategic innovation projects. Insights gained in this part of the literature review can be used to structure the data collection within the investigation in order to understand and explore how innovation work can be (and is) structured in terms of leadership style, culture, team composition, portfolio and risk management, and how creativity is stimulated.

3.6 Strategy, Capabilities, and Key Success Factors

Jaruzelski and Dehoff (2010) state that most of the world's one thousand innovation top spenders belong in one of the three following categories, in accordance with the innovation strategy they pursue:

- **Need Seekers** actively work with their customers, partners, and clients and so on to understand how to develop and offer superior value to the market.
- **Market Readers** watch and analyze market trends and capitalize on proven trends.
- **Technology Drivers** use new technologies to solve problems that are sometimes not articulated; these problems can be either disruptive or lead to improvements.

Organizations need to renew themselves within a contemporary business environment that is especially demanding and characterized by rapid changes in demand, technology, and competition. Innovation is driven by a combination of technological competence and customer competence—that is, a deep understanding of customer insights, customer-appropriate distribution channels, communication, and branding, as well as reputation management (Danneels 2002). The ability to learn about customers and new technology is a critical capability in today's competitive landscape.

Such capability "represents a distinctive and superior way of allocating, coordinating, and deploying resources" (Amit and Schoemaker 1993; Schreyogg and Kliesch-Eberl 2007, as cited by Flynn, Wu, and Melnyk 2010, 247). Moreover, capabilities are company specific, tacit, dependent upon the decision-maker, empirically validated over time, and tend to emerge step-by-step (Flynn, Wu, and Melnyk 2010).

Tovstiga and Birchall (2005) argue that successful innovation is strongly linked to the organizational capabilities of gaining knowledge, learning, and change. They state that "the firm's capabilities are the internal competitive activities with which the firm intend(s)...to fulfill and deliver on the key success factors (related to the specific industry)" (Tovstiga and Birchall 2005, 266). However, not all these capabilities are intrinsic to the firm; the literature suggests that smaller firms tend to outsource their core organizational competencies, while medium-sized firms tend to outsource noncore activities (Haq and Sen 2011).

The drive for radical innovation is related to external factors, internal factors, and specific capabilities. Assink (2006, 219) states that radical innovation capabilities are "the internal driving energy to generate and explore radical new ideas and concepts, to experiment with solutions for potential opportunity patterns detected in the market's white space and to develop them into marketable and effective innovations, leveraging internal and external resources and competencies."

Moreover, Assink (2006) identifies five clusters (or barriers) of key inhibitors of those radical (game-changing) capabilities:

- **Adoption barriers**, where many successful enterprises lose their innovation edge by only focusing on improvements and not working with disruptive innovations and out-of-the-box thinking.
- **Mind-set barriers**, where many firms have problems to unlearn.
- **Risk barriers**, where there is the typical "not-invented-here" syndrome and a focus on old experience and knowledge that was relevant and true in the past.
- **Nascent barriers,** where the company culture fails to motivate people to be innovative and creative as the company grows.
- **Infrastructural barriers**, where at first there are challenges with standards and after-launch challenges with conservatism on the market.

On the whole, the literature suggests that different innovation strategies call for different capabilities and that these capabilities are linked to the fulfillment of *key success factors* (KSF) in the trade. Technology-driven strategies call for a culture of motivation; the ability to unlearn outmoded conventions; tolerance for challenging assumptions; opportunism; a high focus on product life cycle and infrastructural issues; as well as being able to allocate, coordinate, and deploy resources effectively (Tovstiga and Birchall 2005; Assink 2006; Flynn, Wu, and Melnyk 2010; Jaruzelski and Dehoff 2010).

The concept of key success factors can be applied in several ways to the topic of innovation as well; one way is "as a description of the major skills and resources required to be successful in a given market" (Grunert and Ellegaard 1992). KSFs can be divided into perceived and actual key success factors. Perceived KSFs are assessed through interviews, while actual KSFs are measured by collecting objective or semiobjective data that correlates cost and perceived value.

KSFs can be identified within a given industry, a company's competitive strategy, and the firm's market position. If a KSF matches a firm's strength (one of the firm's capabilities), the performance of the firm within the marketplace can be expected to be positive. However, to be successful, the company must be able to deploy its KSF cost-effectively; otherwise it will just be slack (Grunert and Ellegaard 1992).

Tovstiga and Birchall (2005) provide examples of key success factors that include the ability to:

- deliver superior value through products and services;
- carry out competitive manufacturing and commercial process reviews;
- attract superior talents (employees with critical expertise and skills);
- grow the business through competitive pricing and marketing image; and
- establish and maintain a long-term relationship with satisfied customers.

Moreover, Tovstiga and Birchall (2005) also point out that capabilities are not always fully exploited and might have a strong or a weak impact on the performance of the firm.

In their 2010 study of innovative companies, Jaruzelski and Dehoff outline their capabilities (as shown in table 3), noting that, in general, they are more differentiated and have higher margins (EBITDA) and market capitalization relative to their competitors.

Category	Capability
Ideation	- Supplier and distributor engagement in ideation process - Independent competitive insights from the marketplace - Open innovation/capturing ideas at any point in the process - Detailed understanding of emerging technologies and trends - Deep consumer and customer insights and analytics
Project Selection	- Strategic disruption decision-making and transition plan - Technical risk assessment/management - Rigorous decision-making around portfolio tradeoffs - Project resource requirement forecasting and planning - Ongoing assessment of market potential
Product Development	- Reverse engineering - Supplier-partner engagement in product development - Design for specific goals - Product-platform management - Engagement with customers to prove real-world feasibility
Commercialization	- Diverse user-group management - Production ramp-up - Regulatory/government relationship management - Global, enterprise-wide product launch - Product life-cycle management - Pilot-user selection/controlled rollouts

Table 3: The most important innovation capabilities (Source: Jaruzelski and Dehoff 2010).

3.7 The Innovation Process

Managing innovation work is related to uncertainty, and Trott (2008) finds that there can be uncertainty within the process, the outcome, or a combination of the two. For example, application engineering is a typical area of innovative product development that is managed by a well-defined process; in contrast, development engineering is more un-structured but tends to have a well-defined goal. Exploratory research is also referred to as "blue sky" (as it is "up in the clouds" working with new technologies that are not fully understood) with a fuzzy goal or idea of what is to be achieved (Trott 2008).

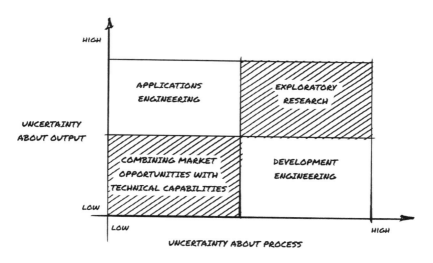

Figure 3: Pearson's uncertainty map (Source: Pearson 1991; cited by Trott 2008).

The literature lacks a generally agreed-upon process for innovation that covers all aspects of innovation management. The most commonly found processes are for new product development, where the general steps are the following:

- Idea generation: initial screening and preliminary assessment
- Definition: market analysis and preliminary financial analysis, decision on business case
- Development

- Postreview
- Validation, including in-house tests and precommercialization decision
- Commercialization
- Postimplementation review

Projects typically have a sponsor and an executive team who make decisions at critical junctures. Often projects are organized in portfolios, which are managed to create maximum impact at a defined level of risk (Tovstiga and Birchall 2005).

The value of innovation, generated within a systematic innovation process, can be measured by applying Key Performance Indicators (KPIs), as shown in table 4. The KPIs are divided into three groups: idea generation, conversion, and diffusion of the innovation (Hansen and Birkinshaw 2007).

Idea Generation			Conversion		Diffusion
In-House	Cross-Pollination	External	Selection	Development	Speed
Do people in our unit create good ideas on their own?	Do we create good ideas by working across the company?	Do we secure enough good ideas from outside the firm?	Are we good at screening and funding new ideas?	Are we good at turning ideas into viable products, businesses, and best practices?	Are we good at diffusing development ideas across the company?
Number of high-quality ideas generated within a unit.	Number of high-quality ideas generated across units.	Number of high-quality ideas generated from outside the firm.	Percentage of ideas generated that end up being selected and funded.	Percentage of funded ideas that lead to revenues; number of months to first sale.	Percentage of penetration in desired markets, channels, customer groups; number of months to full diffusion.

Table 4: Innovation management KPIs (Source: Hansen and Birkinshaw 2007).

When discussing KSFs and determining how to measure and manage them, some useful tools include the generic process steps in Tovstiga and Birchall's stage-gate process at Agilent (2005), the "Innovation Radar" discussed by Mohanbir Sawhney, Robert C. Wolcott, and Inigo Arroniz (2006), and Hansen and Birkinshaw's (2007) KPIs.

3.8 Market Structure and Competition

In 1980, Michael Porter introduced his "Five Forces" framework, in which he introduced the concept that competition comprises five forces: entry of new competitors, threat of substitutes, bargaining power of buyers, bargaining power of suppliers, and rivalry among existing competitors (Porter 1980).

In his subsequent work, Porter (1990, 1996) argued that while competitive advantage is gained by pressure and challenge, *sustainable* competitive advantage is gained based on something distinctive and different within a company, not just excellence in operation and cost cutting, which will always converge within the industry.

More than twenty years after Porter made this case, today's market is global and hypercompetitive, where no competitive advantage is sustainable and all competitive advantage erodes. In order to cope with this hypercompetitive market, companies must actively aim to disrupt not only their rivals' competitive advantages but also their own. To better characterize businesses and markets in today's global market a new model with seven forces—the *7Ss* model—was developed to identify a company's own strengths and weaknesses and analyze an industry and its competitors (D'Aveni 1995). D'Aveni's *7Ss* model is shown in figure 4.

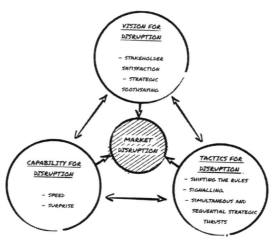

Figure 4: The new 7S's model (Source: D'Aveni 1995).

D'Aveni, Dagnino, and Smith (2010) point out that in a world of hypercompetition, sustainable competitive advantages might not exist anymore, or at least might cease to exist over time and as one single competitive advantage. They comment that temporary competitive advantages are increasing in importance, while perceived sustainable competitive advantages are decreasing in importance, as the market becomes more complex, and it gets increasingly easy to imitate and/or disrupt previous competitive advantages. They suggest using chaos-theory models as well as the theory of complex systems, to deal with this new situation. At the same time, they suggest the possibility that temporary competitive advantages might just be a special case of Porter's five forces, where low barriers to entry and low numbers of new entrants are combined with high power in suppliers and buyers, all of which lead to a hypercompetitive industry rivalry with many short-term competitive advantages. Their conclusion is that firms must build their ability (capability and competence) to search for and adopt temporary competitive advantages while being able to handle multiple strategies to gain and keep market share.

3.9 How to Build the Right Innovation Capability

According to Penker (2016), companies—consciously or unconsciously—develop strategies, leadership, culture, capabilities, and competencies that they use to improve and innovate their business, both internally (e.g., processes) and externally (e.g., value proposition). McKinsey's Steve Coley divides this innovation work into three parallel horizons (McKinsey & Company 2009), each representing a so-called S curve:

- **Horizon 1** (H1) refers to incremental innovation in the current business, which lengthens the existing S curve of the company.
- **Horizon 2** (H2) is about expanding and building new businesses through innovation, thus forming the company's next S curve.
- **Horizon 3** (H3) is an explorative approach to identifying and testing future possible S curves, to be commercialized in H2, and ultimately ending in H1.

O'Reilly and Tushman (2004) propose the latent possibility of working ambidextrously with both incremental and radical innovation. Dividing innovation work into different "horizons" in order to manage it effectively is common knowledge in the business world, particularly among C-level executives. Despite this, however, many companies still prioritize large H1 projects, and the result is numerous projects that frequently create less value for the company.

To counteract this trend, companies could use their common resources optimally to improve and protect their current profit (H1), while simultaneously developing tomorrow's earnings and market share (H2) and learning for the future (H3). This would involve using and developing the leadership, culture, capabilities, and competencies most efficiently and, as advised by Scott, killing the "zombie projects" in H1—those projects that "fail to fulfill their promise and yet keep sucking up resources" (Scott, Duncan, and Siren 2015). To achieve this, companies need to understand how to organize and transform themselves into organizations that are able to work in the short, medium, and long terms, while maximizing their use of both tangible and intangible resources.

The correlations in the data studied by Penker (2016) shown in table 5 indicate that different horizons call for different strategies, leadership styles, capabilities, competencies, and metrics.[1]

Horizon 1. Most companies put their core efforts into H1 (up to 99 percent, according to many studies), which leads to a working incremental/spiral-staircase type of leadership (table 2). Leaders work step by step toward well-defined goals, calculating ROI, and predicting the future. Capabilities that are typically important for Horizon 1 include having a clear vision, having goal-oriented leadership, coaching around goal setting, focusing and building on the core of the organization, and gaining insights into the market.

Horizon 2. This strategy is based on understanding market needs and using technology in new ways, instead of reading the market and

---

[1] Data structure in the InnoSurvey is based on the Innovation360 Framework and is divided into the categories of Why (strategy), What (type of innovation), and How (sixty-six capabilities, four process steps, and ten personas).

responding to it. Crucial capabilities are platform and design thinking,[2] user research, prototyping, ideation, project, and speed. The H2 leadership style is entrepreneurial: challenging the business model (see Cauldron style in table 2); seed-funding external innovation projects and then buying them back (see Pac-Man style in table 2); as well as acting as the gardener of a fertile field (that is, keeping what works while removing what does not). H2 projects are measurable to the extent that managers work with small experiments and prototypes in order to build the base for cash-flow assumptions.

Horizon 3 is explorative in style, investigating needs on a deeper level and using new technologies for disruption. To sharpen future possibilities through external knowledge sharing, open innovation and cocreation become essential. A common management style includes seed-funding external innovation projects and then buying them back (see Pac-Man style in table 2). H3 projects cannot be measured by traditional methods such as ROI; rather, they are about exploration and learning.

---

2 Design thinking refers to creative strategies designers utilize during the process of designing (Vissner 2006).

	Horizon 1	Horizon 2	Horizon 3
Scope	Core business	Growth business	Future business
Strategic focus	Exploit and optimize existing business (incremental innovation)	Expand existing business while simultaneously building new business	Explore options, place small bets on emerging opportunities (radical innovation)
Innovation strategy	Market reader, technology drivers (incremental)	Technology drivers (partly radical) and need seekers	Technology drivers (radical) and need seekers
Leadership style	Spiral Staircase	Cauldron, Fertile Field, Pac-Man	Explorer
Capabilities with a strong correlation to strategy and leadership	Clear vision, goal-oriented leadership, core focus, market insights	Platform and design thinking, prototyping, speed to market, project selection, ideation	External knowledge sharing, cocreation, open innovation, anthropology, technology watch
Competencies	Fully assembled	To be acquired or developed	Requirements uncertain
Metrics	Return on investment	Net present value based on prototyping and hypothesis	Strategic option value based on scenarios

Table 5: Horizon characteristics. Based on the 2008 to 2016 work of Magnus Penker, Ohr, and McFarthing (2013), Jaruzelski and Dehoff (2010), and Loewe, Williamson, and Wood (2001). All data are collected and analyzed in InnoSurvey (2016).

3.10 Study Findings

The InnoSurvey[3] research examined how one thousand companies in sixty-two countries are organized for leadership and strategy-driving innovation, dividing the companies into two groups: Small Medium Enterprises[4] (SMEs) and larger companies.[5] The SMEs place a greater

---

3 InnoSurvey™ is described in chapter 5.
4 One to five hundred employees
5 More than five hundred employees

priority[6] on innovation, possessing a clear vision, ideation, and exploration, and preparing the ground for the development of H2/H3 than their larger counterparts. Larger corporations, on the other hand, perceive their strengths as reading the market (H1) and selecting the right innovation projects (H2).

It is noteworthy that SMEs include a variety of concurrent leadership styles (up to three), while larger corporations tend to be more uniform. The large companies also have a tendency to blend all types of innovation strategies, which is not the case with SMEs.

These data suggest that a large proportion of SMEs adapt easily to the majority of an innovation horizon model but seem to struggle with strategy, most likely due to lack of resources or strategic competencies. Larger corporations differ, in that they tend to set one or several (flexible) strategies and strategic directions, handling uncertainty and many horizons at the same time. On their part, however, larger organizations seem to struggle with multifaceted leadership; their ideas in this regard are more rigid. This can make it difficult for them to work with parallel innovation horizons. From these observations, we conclude that SMEs and larger corporations can learn from each other, with SMEs needing to put greater effort into developing multiple strategies that help to drive innovation work on several horizons and large organizations needing to learn to nurture different leadership styles that support work on several innovation horizons simultaneously.

Penker (2016) points out two more interesting key findings in his research:

- Companies that state that they apply radical innovation also apply incremental innovation, although the converse is not true. This indicates that radicals might be better prepared to handle both certainty and uncertainty at the same time.
- Radical innovators are apparently more developed with respect to innovation management, systematically dividing their work among several innovation horizons. They maintain and nurture

---

6 81.2 percent of SMEs state that they explicitly work with innovation, while 73.3 percent of large organizations explicitly state that they work with innovation.

multiple leadership styles and strategies for optimal resource usage and value creation in the innovation process. See figures 5–7 for background data.

Therefore—based on one thousand assessed companies in sixty-two countries—we conclude that a company applying radical innovation is, generally speaking, better prepared to handle both certainty and uncertainty; simultaneously combines structure and creativity; and systematically builds and aligns the right capabilities, strategy, and leadership to drive innovation in the short, medium, and long term. The result will be risk mitigation, maximization of opportunities, and work proceeding in all three horizons.

Our second conclusion is that SMEs can learn the skill of systematically structuring their work from large organizations. By the same token, large organizations can learn from SMEs to be less rigid and apply the kind of leadership that suits their portfolio of innovation projects best.

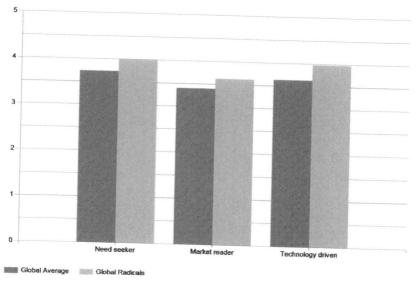

Figure 5: Strategies applied by average versus radical innovators. This graphic demonstrates that global radicals apply more strategies at the same time (on average) than the global average. Based on over one thousand companies in sixty-two countries. (Source: InnoSurvey data.)

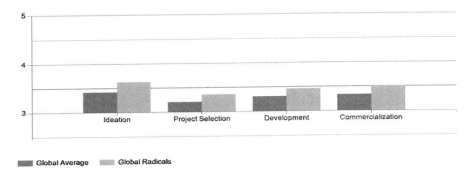

Figure 6: The innovation process applied by average versus radical innovators. This chart indicates that global radicals have stronger capabilities in the four innovation process phases (ideation, selection, development, commercialization), on average, than the global average. Based on over one thousand companies in sixty-two countries. (Source: InnoSurvey data.)

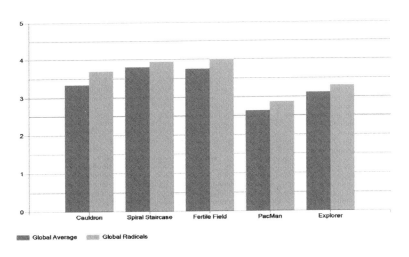

Figure 7: Average number of simultaneous strategies by leadership style. Illustrates that global radicals apply more leadership styles at the same time (on average) than the global average. Based on over one thousand companies in sixty-two countries. (Source: InnoSurvey data.)

3.11 Conclusions

Tovstiga and Birchall (2005) argue that firms use innovation to differentiate themselves based on their capabilities to gain a competitive advantage in the market and that innovation can be seen as based on either internal factors (capabilities) or external factors (i.e., whether an innovation, based on supply and demand, will succeed or not). From this review of current thinking, we have found that innovations can be incremental or radical, and that they may be divided into so-called horizons. We have also seen that there are several kinds of possible innovation strategies, such as those of need seekers, who look for potential opportunities by applying superior understanding of the market and rapid go-to-markets; market readers who capitalize on existing trends and their understanding of their markets; and technology drivers, who drive for breakthrough innovations based on new technology (Jaruzelski and Dehoff 2010).

Several researchers (e.g., Kelly and Littman 2005; Coyne, Clifford, and Dye 2007; Penker 2016; Loewe, Williamson, and Wood 2001) posit that capitalization of internal capabilities is dependent upon leadership style, capabilities as well as the personalities of the people, and the culture of the organization. Moreover, Jaruzelski and Dehoff (2010) suggest that each strategy calls upon different capabilities for success.

The capabilities for success (or KSFs) can also be divided into actual and perceived KSFs (Grunert and Ellegaard 1992). *Actual KSFs* are those that by certainty lead to expected results, while *perceived KSFs* are simply expected to lead to certain results. The literature also discusses several kinds of possible innovations. Trott (2008), for example, describes eight kinds of innovations.

In current thinking, innovation is seen as potentially providing competitive advantages, although some researchers (e.g., Le 2008; Shrieves 1978) caution that there is a dualistic relationship between innovation and oligopolistic market structures, where a competitive advantage will be readily imitated by competitors, requiring the company to innovate repeatedly and yielding less growth than in a market with more competition and/or a larger population.

3.12 Study Questions

3-1) Why would you say it is important to innovate in your (or your client's) organization?

3-2) What type of innovation do you think would be most efficient? Why do you think it would be most efficient? What do you mean by most efficient?

3-3) What type of innovation do you think would be least efficient? Why do you think it would be least efficient? What do you mean by least efficient?

3-4) How would you describe the horizons?

3-5) How can the three horizons help you describe and explain risk, timing, and how innovation projects are managed?

CHAPTER 4

THE INNOVATION360 FRAMEWORK FOR ASSESSING AND MEASURING INNOVATION CAPABILITY

Why are some companies more successful than others? Is it coincidence? Do they have a more capable and well-connected board and investors? Is there a superskilled entrepreneur at the helm? Even more importantly, why do certain companies succeed time after time, while others alternately fail or succeed?

To answer these questions, research studies were carried out, first by defining a framework and then by collecting and analyzing data from over one thousand companies in sixty-two countries. This undertaking was the basis for the formation of the Innovation360 Group. The subsequent combination of the measurement framework and the databases was named InnoSurvey and was fully commercialized in 2015. Today, they are used by licensed practitioners[7] all over the world.

The Innovation360 Framework (figure 8) is defined by six fundamental questions, often referred to as "the 5 Ws and the H" of problem solving. The framework is based on the conviction that an innovation process is necessary in order for a corporation to be a world-class innovator. Based on current thinking, it stipulates that there can be five different leadership styles, ten different personas, and sixty-six capabilities (organized in sixteen aspects), all supporting the four different process steps that characterize a well-defined innovation process. Personas, aspects, and innovation process are different perspectives of capabilities.

---

7 Licenced practitioners are trained and accredited in the use of the Innovation Framework and InnoSurvey™ by Innovation360 Group.

We consider the perspectives as seeing the innovation through a lens (e.g., the personas lens and the aspects lens).

The sixty-six capabilities, also inherited from current thinking, are organized into sixteen innovation aspects, as illustrated in the Wheel of Innovation shown in figure 9. The Wheel of Innovation, as an illustration, is inspired by the work of Mohanbir Sawhney, Robert C. Wolcott, and Inigo Arroniz (2006) and is based on the analysis from more than one thousand companies in sixty-two countries, as well as many years of extensive consulting assignments by the authors. The Wheel of Innovation will be explored in greater detail in chapter 4.7 of this volume, and in an even deeper dive in volume 2 of this book series.

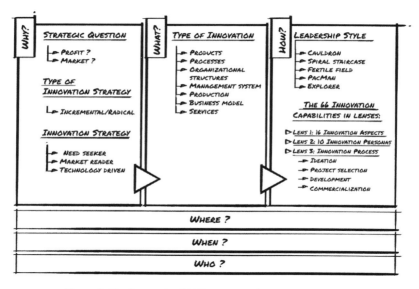

Figure 8: The Innovation360 Framework (Source: Penker 2011c).

4.1 Why Innovate?

The simple question "Why innovate?" leads us to examine the strategic nature of innovation. We know innovation is a strategic necessity, because the purpose of innovation is to ensure that your organization survives, and the evidence overwhelmingly shows that any organization that doesn't innovate probably won't stay in business for long. Hence, the innovation process should be aligned with the organization's strategy, and innovation should be a key factor that defines how the strategy will be realized. The relationship between strategy and innovation, and the condition that they are enabling and driving each other, is an essential cornerstone of the Innovation360 Framework. The *why* questions cover whether the organization aims for profit or growth. In the case of NGOs and NPOs, profit can be interpreted as utilization, for example citizen/member advantage or usage. The *why* questions also address the degree to which the organization focuses on small, incremental improvements or radical innovation, whether the organization is pursuing both at the same time. Finally, the three innovation strategies described in chapter 3 are explored as part of the *why* questions. Defining *why* for the organization will better help answer the *what, how, where, when,* and *who* questions.

4.2 What to Innovate?

When we ask the question "what to innovate," we recognize that the unpredictable nature of change requires us to prepare for many types of innovation options for a wide range of possible futures. Therefore we use the typology introduced, in chapter 3, by Trott (2008) to gain greater specificity about the kind of innovation that is applied. The seven types of innovation are the following:

1. **Product Innovation:** the development of a new or improved product.
2. **Process Innovation:** the development of a new process, for instance a manufacturing process, talent-management process or supply process; typically driven by digitalization, automatization, robotics, artificial intelligence, and new man-machine interfaces such as tablets and smartphones that can be integrated in managing and optimizing processes.
3. **Organizational Innovation:** a new venture division, a new innovation center, internal communication system, and introduction of a new accounting procedure are some examples.

4. **Management Innovation:** examples include TQM (total quality management) systems, BPR (business processes reengineering) and Agile Development for software engineering.
5. **Production Innovation:** quality circles, just-in-time (JIT) manufacturing systems, new production-planning software as well as new, more advanced and technology-related areas such as Industrial Internet of Things (IIoT) used to connect machines to each other as well as to producers, operators, and even customers.
6. **Commercial/Marketing Innovation:** can be new financing arrangements, new sales possibilities, pricing models with low-entry process levels, market approaches (e.g., direct marketing); this can also be referred to as business-model innovation, meaning the development of new or improved business models and value propositions.
7. **Service Innovation:** examples include Internet-based financial services (typically referred to as FinTech), user-experience-based service innovation using new interfaces like virtual reality and augmented reality.

By linking *why* with *what,* we delineate the strategic rationale of the innovation-management work within the organization.

4.3 How to Innovate?

The answer to this question is universal to all companies, large or small, through the essential mechanism of an innovation process. Whatever it comprises, the process must be driven by strategic intent (the *why* of innovation) so the innovation process itself begins with strategy. The second component of the process is the *what* of innovation; this is a highly strategic question and not just happenstance. Many organizations believe that defining the *what* is one of the first steps, when in fact, it takes place in the middle of a strategic, well-implemented innovation process.

In the Innovation Framework, we divide *how* into four components: Leadership, Capabilities, Personas, and the Innovation Process. In chapter 3—"Leadership, Personas, Capabilities and the Innovation Process"—all are described.

The leadership styles in the Innovation Framework are based on the work of Loewe, Williamson, and Wood (2001), who describe five types of leadership such as the following:

1. **The Cauldron:** an entrepreneurial style where the business model is frequently challenged.
2. **The Spiral Staircase:** a style where you climb upward without losing the overall goal.
3. **The Fertile Field:** a style where the organization tries to use existing capabilities and resources in a new way.
4. **The Pac-Man:** a style where you invent, outsource, and finance startups.
5. **The Explorer:** a style where you explore possibilities and invest time and money in them without demanding short-term profit.

The Innovation Personas in the Innovation Framework is based on the Ten Faces of Innovation described in the work of Kelly and Littman. Kelly and Littman divide the ten personas into three categories: learning personas, organizational personas, and building personas. The *learning personas* are individuals digging for new sources and knowledge; the *organizational personas* are the ones structuring, challenging, and orchestrating the work; the *building personas* are typically the intellectual architects, the storytellers, and the caregivers, as well as the ones setting up a proper environment. The ten Innovation Personas are as follows (all described in chapter 3):

1. Persona: **The Anthropologist** (Learning)
2. Persona: **Cross-Pollinator** (Learning)
3. Persona: **Experimenter** (Learning)
4. Persona: **Hurdler** (Organizational)
5. Persona: **Director** (Organizational)
6. Persona: **Collaborator** (Organizational)
7. Persona: **Experience Architect** (Building)
8. Persona: **Set Designer** (Building)
9. Persona: **Storyteller** (Building)
10. Persona: **Caregiver** (Building)

The sixty-six capabilities in the Innovation Framework are organized into sixteen aspects to simplify the analysis (sixteen aspects to analyze instead of sixty-six), and are individually described in chapter 4.7. The Innovation process, consisting of the phases ideation, project selection, and commercialization, are all covered by the Process Aspect in the Wheel of Innovation and will not be further commented upon in this volume. In volume 2, *The Elements of Innovation*, all parts of the Innovation Framework, including the sixty-six capabilities, will be described in detail. In volume 3, the innovation system, including the innovation-process system, will be described in detail.

4.4 Where to Innovate?

An innovation process is realized through the tools and infrastructure that support it and the people who are involved in the process. As discussed in Section 3.4, "Open Innovation," today's innovators need to determine whether their innovation processes will be purely internal or will take some form of open innovation, where stakeholders external to the company or organization are involved in the process. These decisions will determine the innovation infrastructure provided by the company as well as three related elements such as the following:

- The type of innovation (e.g., open innovation, engaging people internally and externally)
- Collaborative platforms to support agile and fast value creation
- The physical workplace (where people are engaged and motivated)

4.5 When to Innovate?

The simple answer here is "All the time!" However, every activity in a business needs to be assessed to fully understand its impact, and this is especially the case for creative work such as innovation. It is imperative to fully understand what is driving value and to measure the work effort and the end results in order to optimize the outcome of the innovation work. In the Innovation Framework, we therefore assume that innovation will take place constantly and at a high pace and that it will be guided and monitored by metrics and coached for value and results.

4.6 Who Innovate?

Who refer to all people participating, internally and externally, in leaving ideas all the way to testing, prototyping, developing and launching them. Typically you organize people into innovation board, innovation task force, sponsors, project leaders an process owners which is described in detail in volume 3 of this series.

4.7 The Wheel of Innovation

The Wheel of Innovation is designed to measure the capabilities of an organization. The sixty-six capabilities defined in the Innovation360 Framework are mapped onto sixteen aspects (legends) in the Wheel of Innovation. Each of these aspects is discussed in detail in the second volume of *The Complete Guide to Business Innovation.*

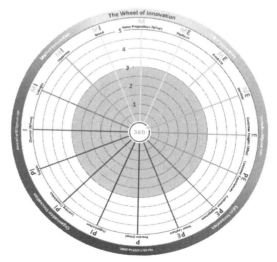

Figure 9: The Wheel of Innovation.

In the Wheel of Innovation, each of the aspects is rated on a scale of 1 to 5:

5 = Changing the Industry (white area)
4 = Strong (white area)
3 = Neutral (between white and gray area)
2 = Weak (gray area)
1 = None (gray area)

The Wheel of Innovation can be used to plot an organization's profile and compare it to other organizations or industries. However, in practice, it has been shown to be unhelpful to base the organization's profile on the input of one or a few individuals' perception of the organization's capabilities. In the InnoSurvey database, analysis of the standard deviation for answers to the same questions (related to the capabilities building up the sixteen aspects of the Wheel of Innovation) has clearly shown that, regardless of the size, trade, geography, or maturity of the organization, perception matters.

Thus, in a major contribution to innovation management, a 360-degree approach was developed by Penker (2011c), so that many perceptions on different levels could be gathered. Over many years of work and analysis of more than one thousand companies in the database, it has become evident that measuring the perceptions of external stakeholders, management, and employees is useful. In practice, a total of one hundred respondents has been shown sufficient to provide deep insights into alignments between internal and external stakeholders as well as between management and employees. In large, especially complex organizations, it has also become evident that the organization needs to be divided into several subgroups beyond just externals, management, and employees. Figure 10 illustrates an example of a measurement where InnoSurvey was used to collect data from more than one hundred respondents, grouped into four internal groups and one external group. Data can be collected through interviews, questionnaires, or more advanced digital solutions such as InnoSurvey. As can be seen in figure 10, there is a large variation in the perception of capabilities, but there are also patterns that can be analyzed and assessed, ultimately generating possible recommendations for the organization. The Wheel of Innovation can also be used for comparison with competitors or other industries, as shown in figure 11.

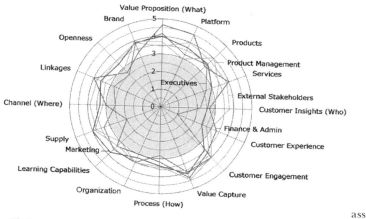

ass

Figure 10. Data from a fast-growing unicorn, based on more than one hundred respondents divided into four internal groups and one external group of stakeholders.

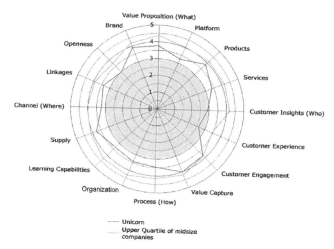

Figure 11. Data from a fast-growing unicorn, based on more than one hundred respondents, compared with midsized companies in the upper quartile.

4.7.1 The Nomenclature

The Wheel of Innovation is composed of four dimensions (see figure 12) such as the following:

- Driving External Transformation (E): These capabilities are linked to external transformation, which relates to the offer and to sales.
- Driving Internal Transformation (I): These capabilities are linked to internal transformation, which relates to the organization and marketing. Marketing refers to building capabilities for growing the market, not market activities, which fall under sales.
- Driving Market (M): These capabilities drive market expansion, which is also supported by data from InnoSurvey.
- Driving Profit (P): These capabilities drive profit, which is also supported by data from InnoSurvey.

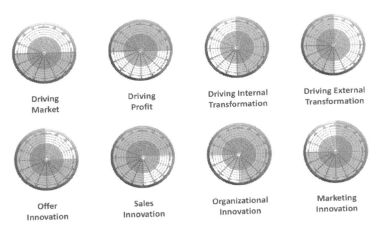

Figure 12. Eight shadows of innovation.

4.7.2 Innovation Aspect: M—Value Proposition (What)

Defining your organization's value proposition is about uncovering what you are really good at—the DNA of the organization—and clearly expressing it, while at the same time attracting the right customers, clients, members, citizens, or other primary target groups. It also requires you to reinforce the offer in every single contact, from lead to sale to aftermarket. The value proposition is essential to driving and expanding the market, and finding the intersection between developing the offer (external context) and building the capability for marketing (internal context). Typically, entrepreneurial organizations score very high here.

4.7.3 Innovation Aspect: M E—Platform

In the first horizon, organizations typically work with incremental innovations, and therefore it is necessary to keep costs and the development timeframe low. By deploying organizational components, blueprints, value offers, and all kinds of documents, including a process description and other useful bits and pieces, it is possible to work with continuous improvements and bring the innovation to market reasonably quickly, while keeping the cost down at the same time. This process is what we call "developing a platform." Typically, it is organized through the use of product life-cycle management systems and other software. The automobile industry is a tangible example where platforms are used to create cost-efficient incremental innovation within the individual organization as well as among organizations creating de facto trade standards.

In the second and the third horizons, platforms focus more on architectural principles, for example in the software industry with its APIs, clean code, and bootstrapping. Technical architectural principles can be used as inspiration for creating platforms in business, driving reuse, standardization of interfaces to create common ground for fast experiments, and innovation at a fraction of the cost compared with large-scale implementations of organizational changes. Large-scale organizational changes are always risky; therefore, conducting small, fast experiments is an alternative that enables the organization to test an idea before scaling up (but that calls for platform thinking to make it possible).

4.7.4 Innovation Aspect: M E—Products

The product-development aspect of an organization concerns whether and to what extent there is a systematic and working product-development process in place (specifically, the development phase of the innovation process) that contains development guidelines, evaluation of competitors' features, and guidelines for planning the market launch. In contrast, the *innovation aspect process* is broader and contains all innovation-process capabilities, while the *services innovation aspect* refers to specific service characteristics. Unlike those two aspects, which are largely internally focused, developing products drives external transformation and market growth.

4.7.5 Innovation Aspect: M E—Services

The service aspect encompasses systematic development and evaluation of existing and new services based on the organization's systematic work to gain customer insights. An example of a company doing this successfully is Netflix, which analyzes the kinds of movies customers order, when they do it, and how they do it (for instance, if the streaming viewer replays a specific scene). Netflix uses these insights to not only generate services like reminders and recommendations, but also for content production. In this way, developing innovative services can cause external transformation that drives market growth. Service design is a discipline that can dramatically improve the productivity and quality of services.

4.7.6 Innovation Aspect: E—Customer Insights (Who)

The organization committed to gaining customer insights studies and analyzes actual customer behavior as well as undertaking frequent independent market research and assessing market potential in order to segment the market in innovative ways. This is typically undertaken by analyzing data from sales, marketing, and customer care as well as running surveys, interviews, focus groups, and field studies. In this way, the organization generates a deep understanding of customer decision-making processes, which can be used to drive external innovation and the development of internal processes to support it. One famous company generating customer insights based on big data and using it in innovative ways is Amazon, which is creating new data-driven customer offerings from cloud computing and AI to book self-publishing services and logistics.

4.7.7 Innovation Aspect: Innovation Aspect: P E—Customer Experience

An organization innovating based on customer experience uses an anthropological approach to studying human behavior in order to gain accurate new customer insights. This data-gathering process is typically not pursued though direct interaction but rather through watching and learning. This type of organization builds in automatic evaluations of how customers use and experience innovations, which it can then analyze to determine its next step. It also carries out regular A and B testing of new innovations, systematically comparing customer reactions to variants of the same innovation. Customer experience drives customer loyalty and yields fewer complaints, higher utilization, and ultimately sustainable profit. One of the most well-known firms using this approach is Gillette, which has employed anthropologists to study human behavior and needs on a deeper level. As a result, it has maintained its market position and price level over time (although its competitors offer similar-quality products at cheaper prices).

4.7.8 Innovation Aspect: P E—Customer Engagement

Engaging customers and stakeholders is among the most efficient ways to create sustainable relationships and gain insights on a deeper level than ordinary market research. In this innovation aspect, building a community and involving them through activities such as cocreation, ideation, and rewards is key. Typical industries using this approach are the gaming industry, which encourages mods (modification by users), the software industry, with its open-source communities like Linux and commercial platforms such as LEGO MINDSTORMS® OS, and Unity, the leading platform for developing computer games. LEGO, Spotify, and several other companies also have open web pages for engagement around innovation (so-called innovation playgrounds), including https://ideas. lego.com and https://community.spotify.com.

4.7.9 Innovation Aspect: P E—Value Capture

Capturing and protecting value is essential in the first and some of the second horizons, where commercialization and market penetration are essential. Intellectual property (IP) protection is one component of value capture, but at least as important is claiming a position and visualizing the advantages of being a customer. Proper pricing is important: the organization must develop a pricing system that supports each phase of the offer life cycle, often starting high and decreasing over time. The fashion industry is one of the best examples, where IP protection is secured through trademarks and customer advantages visualized through branding activities such as marketing, product development, retailer and e-shopper involvement, product placement, and customer engagement through, for example, VIP events. The pricing is carefully thought through, starting high and decreasing systematically, until the product ends up in low-price outlets when the season is over. This aspect is highly linked to profit and is concerned mainly with external factors.

4.7.10 Innovation Aspect: P—Process (How)

In the context of innovation, the process aspect refers to the complete innovation process—from idea generation, prototyping, a system for project selection, R and D cost control, speed to market, piloting, test methodology, ramp-up mechanism, and risk assessment to analyzing and handling market regulations and management of the complete product life cycle. Typically, the innovation process is linked and adopted depending on the innovation horizon and the company's mix in the innovation portfolio. This aspect is linked strongly to profit and is both internally and externally focused. Examples of successful companies running best-in-class innovation processes are IBM and Google, both of which drive highly efficient innovation portfolios. The gaming industry is far ahead here as well. However, most companies—even successful ones—lack a culture where learning takes place among the different innovation projects within the different strategic initiatives (as also in different horizons).

4.7.11 Innovation Aspect: P I—Organization

Here, the term "organization" is used to describe the organization's ability to deliver innovation projects. Capabilities that are especially important to this aspect are engaging and involving people, supporting goal-oriented leadership with a clear vision, and setting a high priority on innovation in all horizons. Idea diffusion within the organization and cross-functional capabilities, together with talent management and reward systems for innovations, are especially important. Well-known examples of best-in-class organizations for this aspect are Procter & Gamble and Fast-Moving Consumer Goods (FMCG). This aspect is internal and typically drives profit.

4.7.12 Innovation Aspect: P I—Learning Capabilities

Learning is essential to innovation on several levels. Critical capabilities like being opportunistic, involving C-level management, running cross-disciplinary learning, evaluation, and a reward system are essential. Gaining insight from the horizon tree is especially crucial to succeeding in horizons one and two. Well-known large corporations operating in all three horizons and rewarded for their learning efforts include IBM, MindTree, and Verizon. In general, learning is an internal activity and is highly linked to profitability.

4.7.13 Innovation Aspect: P I—Supply

Supply development concerns scanning and involving suppliers and partners in order to extend the core business that you are really good at. Great examples are e-tailers such as Amazon and Alibaba. Typically, today's organizations go about this by defining new digital solutions, new business models, and new ways of producing and delivering offers to the market through digital trading places. One interesting example is CellMark, a $3 billion firm operating in thirty countries that has transformed its business model from being a trader to acting as a global meeting place for entrepreneurs, connecting local producers through digital platforms with distributors all over the world. The supply-innovation aspect is internal and strongly linked to profit.

4.7.14 Innovation Aspect: I—Channel (Where)

The channel aspect is one of the most important to finding new ways of building the capability to interact with the outside world. It is also one of the hardest to expand and develop, as it is not obvious during the emerging phase. Channel development is about how the offer is consumed, how it is distributed, and its delivery format. For instance, in the computer-gaming industry, the digital platform Steam is the most important channel; in the past, the critical channel was brick-and-mortar game stores. On Steam, game-development companies deliver their games electronically and are paid directly by the consumer (a new channel for distribution); the format is new (downloadable and online-connected instead of single-player and based on DVD or DC technology); and it is consumed by adding modifications or actually producing own (by the consumer) modifications (so-called "mods"). We can foresee a shift in the channels here, most likely from actors like Apple and Apple TV or new communities with large numbers of users. But to succeed, new channels cannot just add distribution; they also have to find new ways of consuming the products or services, maybe by adding machine learning or through new technical formats like VR and AR.

4.7.15 Innovation Aspect: M I—Linkages

The linkages aspect is a broad concept that encompasses building and utilizing so-called "echo systems" for developing, engaging, and rewarding external parties, benchmarking, reverse-engineering existing solutions, watching and learning about new technology in order to be faster, increasing capacity, and ultimately mitigating risks to keep the speed-to-market rate high. This kind of multifaceted echo system is one of the most efficient ways of working in parallel in all three horizons, from incremental innovation to radical technology-driven innovations, even with scarce resources. Linkages increase the size of a company's reachable market and are built upon internal strength in identifying, collaborating, and exchanging innovations with outside parties.

4.7.16 Innovation Aspect: M I—Openness

Openness is not about being uncommercial; it is about setting the stage for creating together, learning together, and eventually protecting IP together through patent exchange. One highly successful project of this kind has been WordPress, the most installed CMS (content management system) in the market, with many third-party products distributed and sold through the platform. Other well-known examples are MySQL and LEGO MINDSTORM, with hundreds of thousands of engineers all over the world contributing to a commercial solution sold to households and schools globally. The openness aspect typically contributes to growth of the market and is based on internal changes and development of capabilities for opening up and sharing.

4.7.17 Innovation Aspect: M I—Brand

The aspect "brand" addresses the activities of generating demand, sharing through telling, and setting the stage for creating so-called diffusion of new innovations. One industry that was very successful in this aspect in the recent past was the smartphone industry, which was able to generate demand for new products through new standards and ecosystems (like the App Store), by setting the scene (through resellers and operators), and also through storytelling (media, product placement, etc.), quickly getting their new phones and new functions out on a massive global scale. This aspect is also used well by the experience industries, such as resorts, movies, gaming, and the music business. It is used for generating and growing the market and is built upon primarily internal activities and capabilities.

4.8 Study questions

4-1) Why do you think it is important to *measure* and *assess* innovation characteristics?

4-2) What can you gain from measuring and assessing innovation characteristics in your (or your client's) organization?

4-3) When measuring and assessing *strategy*, how can you use the results?

4-4) When measuring and assessing *leadership*, how can you use the results?

4-5) When measuring and assessing the *type of innovation*, how can you use the results?

4-6) When measuring and assessing capabilities (the sixteen aspects of the Wheel of Innovation), how can you use the results?

CHAPTER 5

ASSESSMENT AND MEASUREMENT

I n chapter 4, we asked why some companies are more successful than others. To answer this question, we conducted some research by first defining an analytical framework and then collecting data from over a thousand organizations in sixty-two countries. The resulting framework and databases—collectively called InnoSurvey—was fully commercialized in 2015 and includes functions for deep, interactive analysis as well as a comprehensive survey engine with a predefined questionnaire available in all major languages. Today, InnoSurvey is used by licensed practitioners all over the world. (To become a practitioner licensed to use InnoSurvey, apply for accreditation at www.innovation360.com.)

It is possible to use the Innovation360 Framework (figure 8) as well as the Wheel of Innovation (figure 13) without any support tools, typically in educational situations. Assessing and measuring innovation manually in real-world assignments is not an especially practical approach, however, which is why we recommend that business consultants become accredited in the use of InnoSurvey.

The purpose of collecting, measuring, and analyzing data about an organization's innovation strategy, leadership, type of innovation, capabilities, and personas is to develop evidence-based recommendations on overall organizational design that will ensure successful implementation of an innovation system (governance, process, detailed organization). This work also prepares the practitioner to coach organizations around making innovation happen.

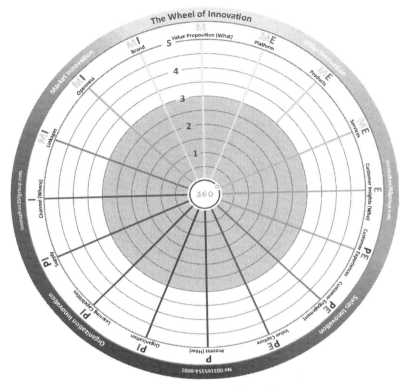

Figure 13: The Wheel of Innovation.

5.1 What Does It Mean to Assess and Measure Innovation?

A dictionary definition (Webster's 1992) of "measure" is to discover the exact size or amount of something and assess, judge, or decide its amount, value, quality, or importance. We use the same semantics. To "measure innovation" is to determine the objectively observable units of a relevant innovation concept, while assessing it is the process of judging how, for a specific organization, those measured concepts are understood and used in the organization and how strong or weak they are in relation to other organizations.

After the data has been collected and measured, organizations and innovation practitioners often rush to define benchmarks as they enter the assessment phase. At this point, a question will often arise: "How will a benchmark of innovation characteristics help you perform innovation management better than the rest of your industry?" To answer this question, ask yourself another: "If you want to perform better than your competitors, should you benchmark against them or against players in other trades, geographical regions, or size cohorts?" Clearly, the answer is the latter.

Thus, after considering Blue Ocean and other strategies for growth, you should define your own sweet spot in the market, build on your own strengths, offer products, and organize your business in ways that others cannot. Benchmarks are still of interest, but only when they enable you to compare your progress to other industries, geographies, and organizations sized differently than your own. Making comparisons with similar organizations will not help you make real leaps. To innovate, it's more important to assess what's possible than to compare yourself to what similar organizations are doing. Moreover, the understanding and use of strategies, leadership, and capabilities are far more effective than just benchmarking. (For theoretical and research background, see chapter 3.9, How to Build the Right Innovation Capability for Innovation.) Benchmarking (focus: comparison), alignment (focus: understanding), and correlation (focus: usage) will be discussed later in this chapter.

5.2 Perception

Before diving into a deeper understanding of benchmarking, alignment, and correlation, the concept of *perception* needs to be elaborated. When analysis is crucial to realizing that we work with people, it is also of paramount importance that we realize it is their *perception of a situation* that we receive in response to a surveys and interviews. The same reality will be perceived differently by the respondents in a survey and an interview. In this section, you will get the theoretical background and advice on how to organize your work for the best results. So, to begin with, let's explore the central concepts of perception and communication before we dig into the analysis itself.

The scientific discipline of *semiotics* (from Greek: σημειωτικός or *simiotikos*) studies the process of making meaning. This includes the study of signs and sign processes (semiosis), indication, designation, likeness, analogy, allegory, metonymy, metaphor, symbolism, signification, and communication. The semiotic tradition explores signs and symbols as a significant part of communications, which create understanding and help us make decisions based on our intent. Thus, unlike linguistics, semiotics also studies nonlinguistic sign systems and is therefore useful when using frameworks like the Innovation360 Framework for innovation management. According to Eckhard D., Falkenberg, E., Hesse W., Lindgreen, P., Nilsson, B.E., Han Oei, J.L., Rolland, C., Stamper, R.K., Van Assche, F.J.M., Verrijn-Stuart, A.A., & Voss, K. (1998) and the highly comprehensive Framework of Information System Concepts Report (FRISCO), communication—that is, the smallest pieces we use to build our understanding, individually and collectively—can be divided into two groups such as the following:

- Physics, empirics, and syntactics, which, when taken together, constitute a domain where technical and formal methods are adequate.
- Semantics, pragmatics, and the social domain.

In the first of these groups, the physical layer is the physical appearance, the media, and the amount of contact available. The empirical layer is the entropy, variety, and equivocation encountered. The syntactical layer is the language, the structure, and the logic used. In the second, the semantic layer is the meaning and validity of what is expressed, while the pragmatic layer is the intentions, responsibilities, and consequences behind the expressed statements. The social layer comprises the interests, beliefs, and commitments shared as a result of communication. Eckhard and his colleagues (1998) explain:

"The natural sciences, and to a lesser degree, the social sciences, as such, deal with reality by making predictions about the outcome of experiments, often in some probabilistic sense. In the information field (Ed. note: for instance, when collecting data regarding innovation characteristics) on the other hand, there is the problem that many of its representations are subject to personal interpretation. However, numerous facts in society only hold true because they have been agreed, such as the value of money, the validity of a marriage or the legality of the government. These might be considered institutional facts, which only concern reality to the extent that they resulted from some societal negotiation."

Some basic business and innovation concepts can be considered as institutional facts, but not the details concepts used to measure and assess innovation. Therefore, it is essential to collect the personal interpretations (perceptions) of many people and also understand the intent of the organization as well as the agendas of the various stakeholders.

Human beings are able to form conceptions in their minds, as a result of current or past perception, by means of various cognitive or intellectual processes, such as recognition, characterization, abstraction, derivation, and/or inner reflection. The collection of (relatively) stable and (sufficiently) consistent conceptions in a person's mind is called his or her knowledge.

Out of one specific perception, human beings can in principle construct any number of conceptions. Figure 14 shows an example. The assumption is that a person sees something which looks like this picture, and has no chance to investigate it further (e.g., by changing the viewing angle). In this case, the person will probably interpret what he or she sees (this specific pattern, a perception) as (at least) two possible conceptions (a wineglass or two faces). In most cases, a single human being is constructing out of one perception exactly one conception at a time. In case of various interpretations of a particular perception, human beings will usually try to resolve those interpretation conflicts by further investigating the domain and will try to get further perceptions thereof. It may be desired, but it is by no means guaranteed, that different people construct out of presumably one and the same perception exactly one and the same conception. Resolution of those interpretation conflicts between different people will usually be attempted by communication (Eckhard et al 1998).

Figure 14. Is it one wineglass, or is it two faces? This is a classic question of perception.

One possible way to deal with different perceptions is to measure the perception of a relevant number of people. Measuring people's perception through the use of surveys will yield a data series that can then be analyzed by calculating the averages and the standard deviation. (Standard deviation will be defined and further explored in chapter 5.8, which addresses alignment.) The averages tell you what the perception is on average, which is interesting if it is a very high or a very low score but less interesting if it is in the middle of the data range. Therefore, *standard deviation* is useful to explore whether and to what extent the respondents do not agree (in their perception). Typically, people working very closely in teams agree more than people working in different teams; the same pattern appears between management and employees and between internal staff and external stakeholders. In many cases, management also has a very different perception, most likely because they do not work as a team, but rather report their results individually to the CEO. The degree to which perceptions within teams and among teams are congruent is what we call *alignment within an organization.*

When setting up a survey and running the data collection (*polling*), the respondents are divided into a number of groups (see "Survey Design for Complex Assessments") in order to compare and contrast different groups' perceptions. Respondents are typically grouped based on perspective and function. Perspective is either external or internal, and internal perspective is further broken down into *overall* (management) or *specialized* (employee). The function groupings are typically brand, process, task, market, and units.

But there is an inherent problem with surveys: the respondent must understand the questions. There are a number of recommended methods for addressing this issue such as the following:

1. Validate the questionnaires by testing many respondents, analyzing their perception, and adjusting the questions.
2. Give explanations within the questions (if necessary).
3. Make sure the questions are available in the local languages spoken by the respondents.
4. Offer an alternative "I do not know" and "Not applicable" (see figure 15 for an example).
5. Use a scale where the respondent must take a standpoint, without the option of choosing a neutral response (for instance the Likert Scale, as shown in figure 15).

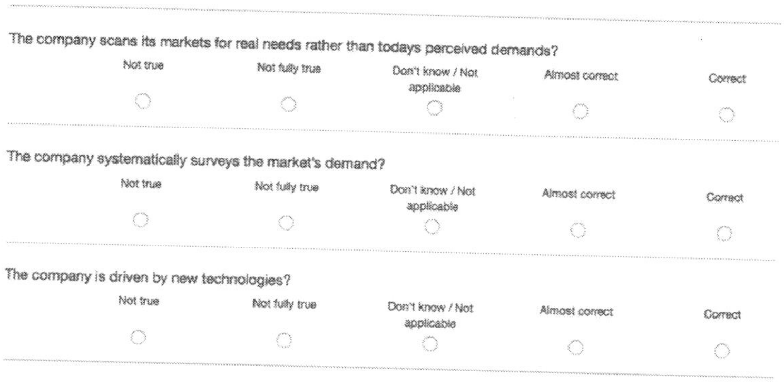

Figure 15. Example of using the widely accepted extended five-degree Likert Scale to pose survey questions.

5.3 Types of Assessment

An assessment is made by collecting data from respondents using surveys, interviews, field studies, or other sources of information, and then measuring it by using a conceptual framework and applying units of measurement to the responses. In this way, the assessment is the process of judging and analyzing the data collected, while the measurement is the process of expressing all data using the same units, making it possible to assess through comparison and contrast and finding similarities, differences, or patterns.

These data are typically collected through one of the following techniques:

- Workshops
- Interviews
- Field studies
- Surveys: individual, team, and organizational assessments

These data are collected based either on a conceptual framework, with or without defined questions, or with an open approach in which there are no defined questions and possibly not even a defined conceptual framework. In innovation assessments of an organization, enhanced practicality has been observed through the use of well-defined and validated questionnaires based on a common conceptual framework, in many languages and completed by many respondents. This way, the assessment can be well structured by comparing, contrasting, and finding patterns even in very large quantities of data.

However, open questions and observations are useful for explaining and communicating interesting key findings and are therefore recommended as a complement to data collection through structured interviews and surveys. The example below comes from a real-world consulting assignment.

Example: A large brick-and-mortar reseller of consumer electronics wants to find a way of increasing gross margin and therefore decides it needs to become more innovative. The assignment starts with interviews of management and store employees and field studies in the stores.

Then an InnoSurvey is conducted among the employees, management, and external partners, such as suppliers of goods and retail interiors. The survey shows clearly that neither the employees, management, nor external parties score high on customer insights (making it harder to innovate for higher value, leading to higher gross margins).

Now, there are three typical responses to this finding: (1) Management does not believe it or downplays its importance; (2) management accepts it and designs a training program for immediate implementation; or (3) management wants to know more and conducts a root-cause analysis before taking any action. Management teams often go for the first alternative, saying either that "people didn't understand the questions" or "if we did this on a larger scale, we would get different results." Denial is a natural reaction. If, however, you provide real observations and quotes from interviews along with the key findings, you will most likely get the second or third reaction. So, as you conduct the interviews and field studies of this assignment, you could package them together with the key findings.

In this case, in the interview with the purchasing management team, we learned that the number of accessories per sold unit (computers, phones, tablets, etc.) was under two, and this was perceived as a problem. The head of accessories said, "I think that the sales representatives get too little training, as they give wrong advice to customers buying our units, and also don't know the assortment, which is clear to me as there are only two accessories sold per unit when others have two and a half." Now, you could stop there, or you could decide to do field studies in the store. In this example, field studies were carried out, and it was discovered (and documented) that the sales representatives in the stores were not trained in understanding their target group. In this case, that target was "prosumers," that is, professionals willing to pay extra for speed and service. One quote came from a customer buying a laptop, who asked, "Is there anything more I can use or buy, anything I missed?"

The sales representative replied, "Yes, a bag would be nice."

The customer said, "I already have a bag." And the sale was closed.

The sales representative could have asked how the customer used the computer and then suggested traveling converter kits, protection film for the screen, an extra power adapter for the office, cables for charging the phone, and so on.

This example illustrates the gap between the perceptions of the sales representative and the customer, and it also provides management with a clear example of the lack of customer insight; its pairing with the interview with the purchasing manager then puts it into a managerial and financial context. In this case, the result was not only a training program but also a complete root-cause analysis in order to understand how the organization could gain more insights and systematically implement a program to innovate new services, processes, and experiences for customers.

5.3.1 Assessments in Workshops

Doing assessments in conjunction with (usually just before) or during a workshop is highly efficient, especially at the beginning of an assessment of the whole organization. Typically, you start with one part of the organization—a subsidiary, business unit, or market—to learn more and create a reference for the rest of the organization. An alternative is to run a workshop with a separate team—a management team, product-development team, digitalization group, on site or at a specific line in production. In the workshop, it is important to establish a common goal for the process and engage the participants in interactions while delivering some key insights. The benefit of doing an assessment in advance is that it helps ensure that the workshop is well prepared and that the right questions are posed. The disadvantage is that the respondents can have difficulty answering the questions in the survey, not necessarily because of the questions themselves but because of the context and internal politics. By running through the survey during a workshop, you can monitor the process, making sure that the context and purpose are clear. At the same time, you can use it as an opportunity to identify internal champions who can be used as sponsors and mentors later, when surveys are administered to a wider group of respondents in the organization, in order to gain insights across the whole organization or within a segment of it.

Conducting a survey during a workshop requires either very easy-to-use digital solutions (including functions for data analysis in real time) or facilitated discussion where smaller groups present the key findings to each other. Running the survey in advance does not require any specific system, but is, of course, made easier by the use of digital solutions.

5.3.2 Assessments in Interviews

On the other hand, the use of digital tools for an interview is not recommended, as the interview should focus on the respondent. Instead, record the interview and have it transcribed afterward. The questions could either be prepared in advance, based entirely or partly on the Innovation Framework, or the interview format can consist of open-ended questions. The advantage of using prepared questions based on the Innovation Framework is that it makes the analysis easier and enables examples to be prepared to illustrate a situation. The disadvantage is that the respondent will be biased, in that he or she will only give you answers to the questions you pose, and you may perhaps lose insights you had not thought to ask about. For this reason, the recommendation is to start with open-ended questions and then move into more specific questions that are based on the Innovation Framework.

Analyzing interviews with open questions is quite difficult, but there are several methods that can be helpful. We recommend grounded theory as a practical approach for analyzing open questions. According to Wikipedia (accessed May 28, 2017), *grounded theory* is a systematic methodology used in the social sciences that supports the construction of a theory through the analysis of data. This research methodology operates inductively, in contrast to the hypothetico-deductive approach. A study using grounded theory is likely to begin with a question or even just the collection of qualitative data. As researchers review the data collected, repeated ideas, concepts, or elements become apparent and are tagged with codes that have been extracted from the data. As more data is collected and re-reviewed, codes can be grouped first into concepts and then into broader categories.

5.3.3 Field Studies/Research

A practical way of collecting data and insights is to observe real situations directly. In science, there are two main types of observational research associated with technology studies: ethnography and ethnomethodology. Ethnography is the dominant qualitative-research method, developed originally by anthropologists studying the cultures of non-Western societies. It is now used in other fields of social research, such as sociology, management, and human-computer interactions. It aims to produce a detailed description of how a particular social group operates—based on observation of and often participation in—the group. This may be supplemented by interviews (and in our case, surveys) and gathering documents and artifacts. *Ethnomethodology*, on the other hand, attempts to understand how people "get on in the world" by exposing the taken-for-granted rules of interaction in everyday life. It typically involves the detailed analysis of social practices, often through the use of video recordings of particular organizational settings.

When doing field research or more simplified field studies, taking notes, photos, and videos is essential. Typically, the researcher takes four types of notes such as the following:

- **Jot Notes:** Keywords or phrases written down while in the field.
- **Field Notes Proper:** A description of the physical context and the people involved, including their behavior and nonverbal communication.
- **Methodological Notes:** New ideas that occur to the researcher on how to carry out the research project.
- **Journals and Diaries:** Notes that record the ethnographer's personal reactions, frustrations, and assessments of life and work in the field.

Using interviews and field research or studies to explain and illustrate key data findings is a very strong approach. Conversely, by studying and observing and/or interviewing, you will be able to formulate hypotheses based on your notes and possibly find some evidence in the data that backs it up.

5.3.4 Surveys: Individual, Team, and Organizational Assessments

A survey consists of questions in a questionnaire, typically divided into several sections with explanatory text for the respondent. Surveys are distributed in various ways: on paper, or as with InnoSurvey and other tools, through a digital solution with e-mail, tracking, and reminder functions as well as tools for analysis. Surveys can be sent to one individual, a team, an organization, a network of organizations, or at a trade or societal level. A survey always measures self-perception; therefore, it is very important to design a survey with that in mind (see chapter 5.2 on perception as well as the next chapter, which delves more deeply into this topic). Moreover, it is also important to define the different groups to be assessed, as discussed in chapter 5.2 and further elaborated in the appendix (see "Survey Design for Complex Assessments").

5.4 360 Innovation Assessment of an Organization: Structure and How to Collect Data in Practice

When measuring and assessing innovation characteristics (the aspect of the Innovation360 Framework described in figure 13) within an organization, a part of an organization, or a network of organizations, there are often many stakeholders in many places, potentially using several languages. For this reason, InnoSurvey was developed as a practical tool for a task that otherwise would hardly be feasible. This chapter describes the Innovation360 and InnoSurvey approach to surveys, an approach we call *360 degree*—meaning it measures the perceptions of important stakeholders and then assesses the characteristics of the organization, part of the organization, or the network of organizations investigated.

First, the survey needs to be designed. Survey questions need to cover important aspects of innovation management and are therefore developed using the Framework of Innovation, innovation capabilities, and the sixteen aspects discussed in previous sections (see the spider diagram in figure 13) and described in the Wheel of Innovation. In the InnoSurvey tool, each aspect of the Wheel of Innovation is detailed with a number of capabilities (sixty-six in total), which synthesize the past hundred years of thinking in innovation management, starting with

Josef Schumpeter and concluding with modern thinkers like W. Chan Kim and Renée Mauborgne (as briefly discussed in chapter 3).

InnoSurvey is organized into three major sections—Why, What, and How—corresponding to the Framework of Innovation. For each section, there are corresponding questions. There is also an additional initial question asking the respondent whether the organization applies innovation for improvement or large leaps. The reason for this is that if a respondent does not believe that the organization is applying innovative thinking, he or she might have difficulties in answering the questions in the survey (as they refer to innovation). By having a specific question regarding whether or not the respondent perceives if the organization applies innovation for improvement or for large leaps, as an analyst, you will be able to compare and contrast the answers between the one stating a belief that the organization applies innovation for improvement or large leaps and the one stating the opposite. Experience shows that respondents stating the organization applies innovation for improvement or large leaps have fewer questions marked with the alternative "Don't Know or Not Applicable" and are therefore also, generally speaking, better understanding of the organization. However, if many more than 50 percent claim that the organization does not apply innovation for improvement or large leaps, it might be hard to do any innovation analysis. It is then recommended to break up the group of respondents (what we call polls) into smaller groups to see if there are groups claiming that they do work with innovation and groups claiming the opposite. Typically, especially in large organizations, you will find groups claiming they do work with innovation and several groups saying the opposite. By understanding the landscape, you can also use this insight in coming phases when designing transformation plans to help organizations implementing innovation systems and designing organizations to be able to take care of that.

In total, InnoSurvey provides ninety-two possible questions, but you can also post surveys based on the Framework of Innovation and the Wheel of Innovation by using software like SurveyMonkey™ linked to statistical programs like IBM's SPSS. Questions, regardless of solutions used, should be related to the following areas:

- Why: Strategy
- How: Leadership and the sixteen aspects of innovation (each aspect can be detailed with more questions asked)
- What: Type of innovation applied

Using a survey engine is strongly recommended; otherwise the researcher is faced with an extensive and tedious process of gathering and tracking all the responses, getting through spam filters, structuring the data, analyzing it, and generating conclusions and graphs manually.

The procedure for selecting respondents and grouping them into polls or survey cohorts will be covered in the appendix labeled "Survey Design for Complex Assessments."

When sending out surveys, it is imperative that the questions are understood. Therefore, it is recommended that all questions are available in all local languages used by the organization (as described in chapter 5.2).

5.5 Preparing for Assessment within an Organization

Many organizations have different official structures (for example, in matrix organizations) and may also employ people with a wide variety of backgrounds, academic skills, and educational levels. For example, in the textile industry, where the consultant might be assessing a factory unit, a union leader might hold a senior managerial position because she or he was elected to that position. In many of today's organizations, you also typically find knowledge workers who expect to be highly involved and might become skeptical if they feel they have been overlooked in project setup or planning. NPOs, NGOs, and member-owned organizations are other examples of organizations with governance structures and political agendas that need to be taken into consideration.

Large organizations with many managerial levels will also most likely include some survey respondents who fall within the "unconscious incompetence" category in Noel Buch's pyramid model (figure 16) before the assessment; this situation calls for careful, step-by-step preparation of the respondents. In knowledge-intensive, complex organizations (even small and midsized organizations such as hospitals and research centers), people sometimes have their own agendas, theories, or just perceptual confusions (business perspectives on nonbusinesses from people with nonbusiness backgrounds). In these organizations, there is often a greater need to involve and enroll people on more levels and to a greater extent than in other organizations.

Involvement can be secured through kickoff meetings, seminars, and study circles that prepare the organization before an assessment. Small organizations are usually much easier to manage, either by a single skilled consultant or an experienced management team, while complex organizations (and sometimes large organizations) might demand extra attention.

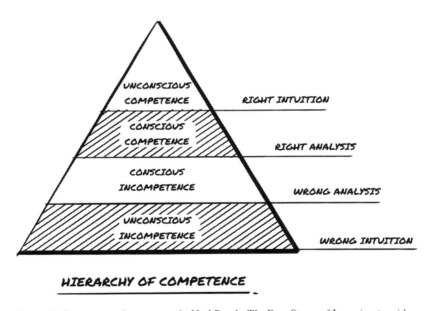

Figure 16: Four stages of competence by Noel Burch. The Four Stages of Learning provides a model for learning. It suggests that individuals are initially unaware of how little they know, or unconscious of their incompetence. As they recognize their incompetence, they consciously acquire a skill, then consciously use it. Eventually, the skill can be utilized without it being consciously thought through: the individual is said to have then acquired unconscious competence (Burch 1978).

In addition to working to secure employee involvement, appointing a sponsor with strong influence can be helpful to the process. You and the sponsor can prepare tools and material to be used, and in very large projects, you can train trainers or coaches to disseminate the material, cascading further down through the organization. Material can consist of workshop materials, discussion templates, and educational material to create a common platform and ensure that all respondents will be able and willing to answer the survey, understand the scope of their cohort, and are ready to be objective when answering. Also, as recommended previously, doing a small on-site assessment before rolling out a larger assessment is one way to engage individuals and prepare the organization. These advance participants can be champions and even coaches in a subsequent rollout.

5.6 Integrate with Business Development

Once an understanding of stakeholders and their perspectives is developed, an assessment of innovation characteristics, combined with a strategic analysis, will form the basis of a highly tangible plan for designing and implementing an innovation system within or among one or several organizational units and/or organizations. The strategic analysis comprises an external analysis, internal analysis, and the generation of options and their evaluation. Once this strategic analysis is completed, the VMOST (see below) framework can be used to express the overall organizational strategy.

> **Vision Statement**: An aspirational description of what an organization would like to achieve or accomplish in the mid- or long-term future. This is intended to serve as a clear guide for choosing current and future courses of action.
> **Mission Statement:** A written declaration of an organization's core purpose and focus that normally remains unchanged over time. Properly crafted mission statements serve as filters to separate what is important from what is not, clearly state which markets will be served and how, and communicate a sense of

intended direction to the entire organization. A *mission* is different from a *vision*, in that the former is the cause, and as for the latter? You could say a given vision serves the organization's mission. An alternative or complement to a mission statement is to define the higher purpose of the organization, based on the core values, that prepares all employees, management, customers, and suppliers for what really makes a difference.

Objectives: The measurable actions you take to fulfill the vision in the mid- or long-term future.

Strategic Direction: The approach and direction you take to achieve the objectives. It is also worth noting that there might be a number of strategies to reach a given objective, meaning that there is not one solution to how to reach the objectives leading to the fulfillment of the vision.

Tactics: The tools you use in pursuing an objective associated with a strategy.

Innovation management is typically linked to possible strategic directions, objectives (or strategic initiatives), and tactics. It is also used to revise the core purpose based on capabilities and competencies.

In the strategic analysis, the external context is typically analyzed using a framework such as Political, Economic, Social, Technological, Legal, Environmental, and Demographic (or PESTLED) for key drivers, and models like Porter's Five Forces for analyzing market characteristics; typically, both the existing and potential market are assessed using these approaches. The external context boils down to identifying opportunities and threats within the market. Internally, both tangible and intangible resources are evaluated: *tangible resources* include capital, facilities, and major equipment; and *intangible resources* are typically patents, copyrights, franchises, goodwill, trademarks, and organizational and structural capital such as processes and organizational structures, competences, and capabilities. This internal analysis yields a catalogue of strengths and weaknesses. The combination of these internal strengths and weaknesses with the external opportunities and threats forms a hunting ground for both incremental and radical innovation opportunities, which provide a set of options from which to choose. Options are then evaluated, typically based on a feasibility-impact analysis. (See figure 17 for an example.)

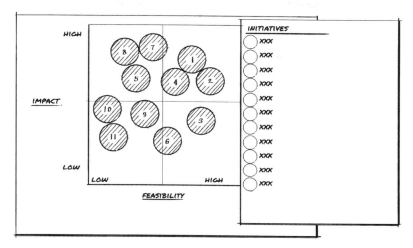

Figure 17. A framework for prioritizing strategic options.

Strategy and leadership, a large topic, will be further explored in the fifth volume of this series.

5.7 Visualizing and Analyzing: Benchmarking

Benchmarking is a way to compare and contrast data sets, typically comparing and contrasting internal data sets with external data sets. We recommend basing the innovation measurement and assessment on the Innovation360 Framework (see figures 14 and 15) by defining a survey with questions relating to each of the elements in the framework (as illustrated in the diagrams shown in figures 20–22):

1. Type of Innovation Strategy
2. Innovation Strategy
3. Innovation Leadership
4. Type of Innovation
5. Innovation Personas
6. Innovation Capabilities

These six diagrams use data from one company (a mean value on a five-point scale) and compare and contrast it to a benchmark data set.

The selection of benchmark data should be based on at least the following principles:

1. It is relevant to what you want to study or the point you want to make in your recommendations. This does not necessarily mean you want to study similar organizations; you could benchmark totally different organizations that are much more successful than their competitors.

2. There is a sufficient number of respondents. In practice, we would argue that anything fewer than one hundred respondents in a benchmark is too few. Make sure not to be too narrow when selecting the benchmark so that the data is sufficient and yields statistically significant results.

In later chapters, we will explore alignment and correlation, which are stronger tools for analyzing innovation characteristics than benchmarking.

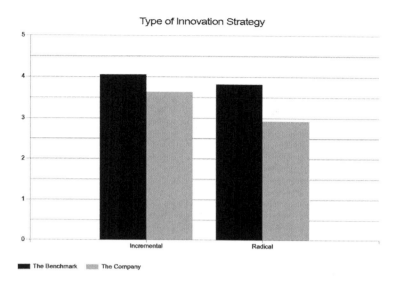

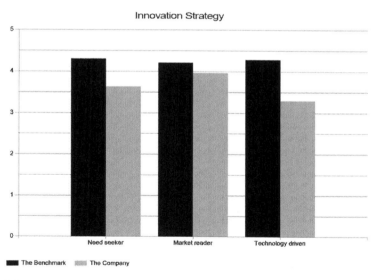

Figure 18: Example of benchmark comparison for type of innovation strategy and innovation strategy.

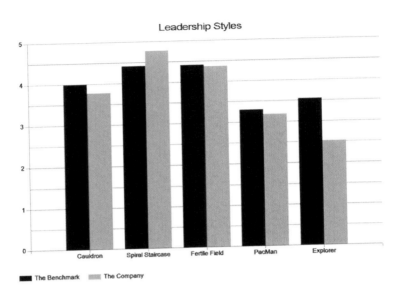

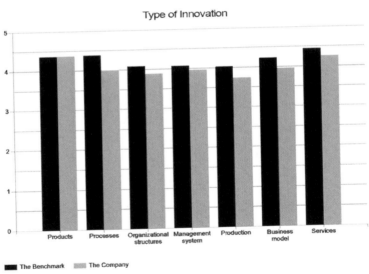

Figure 19: Example of benchmark comparison for innovation leadership styles and type of innovation.

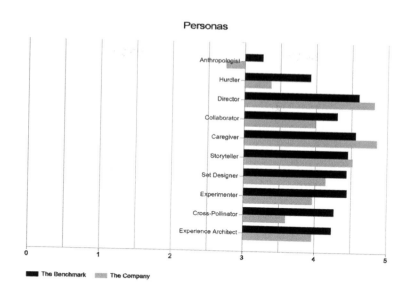

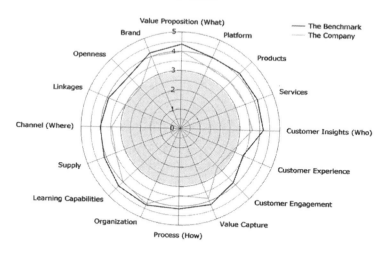

Figure 20: Example of benchmark comparison for innovation personas and capabilities.

5.8 Visualizing and Analyzing: Alignment

When running a survey, it is important to group the respondents into cohorts, not only to compare and contrast among cohorts, but also because large populations will normalize into groups with defining characteristics. But those characteristics are often so generic that they're not useful for trying to characterize target population niches in order to gain insight on a deeper level. When innovation measurement and assessments are undertaken, it is essential to understand both similarities and differences between groups in order to support the later process of identifying solutions.

After the survey is designed, the next step is to identify potential respondents and groups of respondents. Typically, one of the following is used as a "discriminator" (in the distributed-computing sense) for dividing an organization's employees into respondent groups:

- Brand
- Market
- P and L (profit-and-loss statement, meaning dividing respondents based on the part of the P and L they belong to)
- Business Model
- Project (or portfolio of projects)
- Strategic Initiative

Then you typically assign "roles" to them—for example, external, management, or employee—so the survey results will provide different perspectives on the organization or suborganization. (In the appendix "Survey Design for Complex Assessments," we will continue this discussion and describe how to handle more complex situations.)

After responses to the survey have been gathered, you can compare and contrast the data by group to determine how much agreement there is across and within groups. This process measures what we call *alignment* and is one of the most powerful analytical tools available for examining *tacit knowledge*, knowledge that cannot be fully described with written languages, like the innovation characteristics of an organization.

There are three common ways to investigate data sets for alignment among respondents: average value, standard deviation, and frequency. Mean, median, and mode value is useful when comparing groups, because it is simple to communicate. However, it often obscures the real value of the respondents' perception of the questions, as there is often a wide range of responses to a given question. For example, two different groups with the same average response might actually differ greatly; one group might be in complete agreement with each other, while the other might include many respondents with widely differing answers that averaged to a neutral value. For this reason, studying standard deviation and frequency diagrams is a more appropriate approach, since these techniques reveal variation within a group. At the same time, the average says something about the *level* of perception (high or low), so combining the three measurements has been proven to be practical in our consulting assignments. In the next sections, we will walk through standard deviation and frequency tables as well as how to use them in an applied and practical approach to measure and assess the innovation characteristics of an organization.

5.8.1 Standard Deviation

In statistics, the standard deviation (SD, also represented by the Greek letter sigma σ or the Latin letter "s") is a measure that is used to quantify the amount of variation or dispersion within a set of data values. A low or small standard deviation indicates that the data points in a data set (here, the responses to survey questions) tend to be close to the mean value of the data set (meaning, in this case, that the respondents in the group do not differ greatly in their answers). A high or large standard deviation indicates that the data points are spread out over a wider range of values (meaning, in the case of an organizational survey, that the respondents differ more in their perceptions).

A very large standard deviation indicates that the data points can spread far from the mean, while a small standard deviation indicates that they are clustered closely around the mean.

For example, each of the following three data sets has a mean of 7:

{0, 0, 14, 14}
{0, 6, 8, 14}
{6, 6, 8, 8}

Their standard deviations are seven, five, and one, respectively. The third population has a much smaller standard deviation than the other two because its values are all close to seven. Standard deviation is expressed using the same units of measurement as the data points themselves. If, for instance, the data set {0, 6, 8, 14} represents the ages of a population of four siblings in years, the standard deviation is five years. As another example, the data set {1,000, 1,006, 1,008, 1,014} may represent the distances run by four athletes, measured in meters. It has a mean of 1,007 meters and a standard deviation of five meters.

In some contexts, standard deviation may serve as a measure of uncertainty. In physical science, for example, the standard deviation of a group of repeated measurements indicates the degree of precision of those measurements. When deciding whether measurements agree with a theoretical prediction, the standard deviation of those measurements is of crucial importance. If the mean of the measurements is too far from the prediction (where the distance is measured in standard deviations), then the theory being tested probably needs to be revised. This makes intuitive sense, since these measurements fall outside the range of values that could reasonably be expected to occur if the prediction were correct and the standard deviation appropriately quantified.

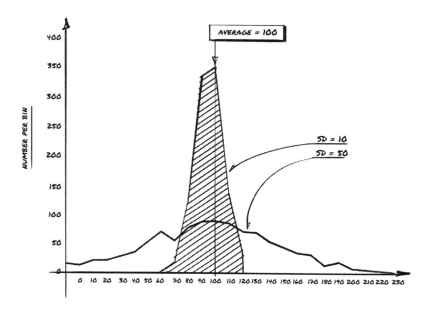

Figure 21. Example of samples from two populations with the same mean but different standard deviations. The population drawn with the shaded area has mean of 100 and SD 10; the population drawn with the line has mean of 100 and SD 50. (Source: Wikipedia, accessed May 27, 2017).

In the case, where X takes random values from a finite data set $x_1, x_2,...,$ x_N, with each value having the same probability, the standard deviation is

$$\sigma = \sqrt{\frac{1}{N}\left[(x_1 - \mu)^2 + (x_2 - \mu)^2 + \cdots + (x_N - \mu)^2\right]}, \quad \text{where } \mu = \frac{1}{N}(x_1 + \cdots + x_N)$$

Measuring and assessing in social science, where you need to consider perception standard deviation, does have its limitations. (Measuring and assessing innovation as a management discipline is comparable to social science.) In a previous chapter, we recommended the use of the extended Likert Scale with the five alternatives from "not true" (1) to "correct" (5) and the middle alternatives of "I do not know" and "Not applicable" (see figure 15 for an example). The reason for this is that you can distinguish perceived true or untrue statements from statements perceived to be not applicable or not known. It is important to point out that innovation assessment on one organization is based on a respondent's perception and level of knowledge. The work by Burch (1978) illustrated in figure 16 suggests that individuals are either initially unaware of how little they know or unconscious of their own incompetence. As they come to recognize their incompetence, they consciously acquire a skill and then consciously use it. Eventually, the skill can be used without being conscious of it. Standard deviation and mean value are not the best ways to determine who agrees, does not agree, or does not know or think a statement is applicable; seeing the spread of the data in the data set might be more helpful to understanding than calculating the mean or the standard deviation.

An alternative to assessing a five-point Likert scale with the neutral option "I do not know" and "not applicable" is to use a frequency table (see section 5.8.2) or to complement it with mean, minimum, and maximum values that provide a better understanding of the spread and alignment. For example, it might be of interest if many respondents scored a question low (even if the mean value is high) and the standard deviation not alarmingly high, as this might indicate misalignment, mistrust, or in some cases, different common-value sets within the organization.

Let's look at InnoSurvey data from a global beverage company, compared to midsize (five hundred to five thousand employees) and large organizations (more than five thousand employees) in sixty-two countries as an example. This company operates in an industry where you can expect high anthropological knowledge compared with, say, the IT industry. Figure 22 shows that they score higher on anthropological personas than the benchmark group of midsize and large organizations worldwide (3.5 compared with 2.39; see figure 23). They also have a reasonably low standard deviation of 1.256 (see figure 23), but they have also one or more employees scoring "1" (not true), which is interesting. How is it possible that a very successful global beverage company claims that, on average (and with reasonable standard deviation), they study human behaviors (which is common in this industry), while one or several employees clearly state they do not? Is it because they are unconsciously incompetent—or do they just have a different perception?

You could investigate whether they are unconsciously incompetent or have a different perception by interviewing respondents (or running formal competence tests), but it is also possible by studying the number of "3" responses (indicating ether unconscious incompetence or the perception that the question is not relevant) as well as the number of "1" (not true) or "5" (correct) responses. Opposite perceptions (even if there are only a few) indicate misalignments if very few respondents choose "3" (I do not know/Not applicable). This indicates that the organization most likely is conscious, since the respondents clearly choose to agree or disagree, not using the alternative "3" response. On the other hand, if many choose "3" as a response, it is most likely an unconsciously incompetent organization (with respect to the particular question), and therefore, it is hard to interpret the response accurately. By studying the predominance of "3" responses, you will be able to understand the level of competence and be able to analyze the response.

Now, some readers might remember that "3" also means the alternative "Not applicable," which is absolutely correct. But we also recommend including a check-box (yes/no) question in the survey that asks whether or not the organization applies innovation. By using this question to divide the respondents into two groups—*innovators* (people who say the organization innovates) and *noninnovators* (those who say it does not)—it is possible to interpret a "3" response by an innovator to mean "Do not know" while a "3" response from a noninnovator can mean either "Do not know" or "Not applicable." The reason you most likely can interpret the "3" as unconscious incompetence if the respondent also claims the organization does apply innovation is because the suggested framework for the survey is based on the current thinking in innovation management, meaning it is, by definition, a relevant question. Furthermore, data from InnoSurvey clearly indicates that the number of "3" responses among innovator respondents is much less than the number of "3" responses from noninnovator respondents.

The discussion in this chapter has shown why we study average, standard deviation, min, max, and frequency of "1," "3," and "5" responses. The next chapter will discuss the concept of frequency tables, a method for studying the spread of a question's responses.

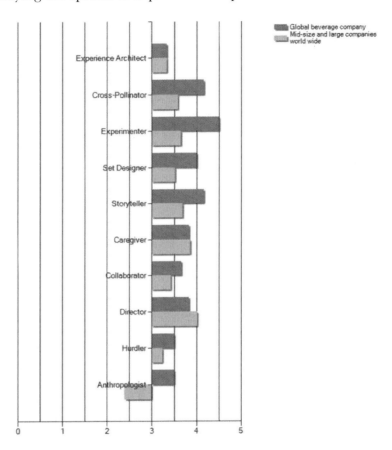

Figure 22. Persona data from a global beverage company and InnoSurvey. The benchmark is midsize (500–5,000 employees) and large organizations (more than 5,000 employees) in sixty-two countries.

Capability / Question	Min	Max	Mean	S.dev
Experience Architect	2/1	4/5	3,33/3,33	0,75/1,2
Cross-Pollinator	3/1	5/5	4,17/3,58	0,69/1,13
Experimenter	4/1	5/5	4,5/3,65	0,5/1,13
Set Designer	4/1	4/5	4/3,52	0/1,14
Storyteller	3/1	5/5	4,17/3,69	0,69/1,17
Caregiver	3/1	5/5	3,83/3,86	0,69/1,09
Collaborator	2/1	5/5	3,67/3,43	0,94/1,1
Director	3/1	5/5	3,83/4,02	0,69/1,08
Hurdler	2/1	5/5	3,5/3,24	1,12/1,07
Anthropologist	1/1	5/5	3,5/2,39	1,26/1,29

Figure 23. Persona data from a global beverage company and InnoSurvey. The figure shows min, max, mean, and standard deviation. The first value in each column is data from the global beverage company and its respondents on the management team; the second is the value from midsize (500–5,000 employees) and large organizations (more than 5,000 employees) in sixty-two countries.

5.8.2 Frequency Tables

After the discussion in the previous section, it might be tempting to think that studying frequencies is the best and only solution, but frequency tables are problematic, as they do not provide mean, min, max, and standard deviation statistics. Dealing with large numbers calls for such computable techniques. However, when something stands out, it is illuminating to dig into the actual data sets, and this is where frequency tables are very useful.

Figure 24 illustrates how the responses in the global beverage company case can be plotted out by the frequency of the responses between one and five. It is clear that the company has an anthropological capability, but when 17 percent claim they "do not know" and 17 percent say that they "absolutely do not have it," there is some doubt. The data shown in figure 24 is only from innovator respondents in an industry where anthropologist personas are actually hired, and anthropology is not just a capability built within the company; therefore, there might be some unconsciousness awareness in the company and possibly some misalignment or different levels of ambition. As this specific company is a need seeker and anthropological personas have a strong impact on that strategy (since anthropologists study human behavior), this is a typical situation calling for further investigation and possible recommendations. In a situation like this one, you typically conduct complementary field research, interviews, and observations related to the data's key findings, in order to form recommendations to improve processes for innovation, training programs, and on-site coaching.

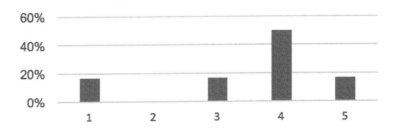

Figure 24. Response shown as a frequency table to the anthropologist persona question by respondents from a global beverage company. The reasons shown as a frequency table.

5.9 Visualizing and Analyzing: Correlation

Correlation is a measure of the linear relationship between two variables (representing data sets) X and Y, giving a value between +1 and −1 inclusive, where 1 is total positive correlation, 0 is no correlation, and −1 is total negative correlation. In innovation assessment and measurement, correlation can be used to develop understanding about the relationships among the different aspects of the Innovation Framework, particularly with respect to the *why*, *what*, and *who* questions.

A practical example based on data from InnoSurvey is shown in tables 6 and 7. Table 6 shows the correlation between the leadership style Spiral Staircase and the sixty-six capabilities measured within InnoSurvey, and particularly the correlation to Clear Vision and Goal Orientation. Table 7 shows clearly that the Cauldron leadership style is correlated to the capabilities Idea Diffusion, Innovation Priority, and Systematic Service Innovation, for example, which seems logical for this style.

While it is very interesting to analyze correlations, they present only a view of the past. Correlation is not performance; rather, it is an indicator of underlying characteristics and therefore more appropriate to extrapolate in an analysis based on history. Understanding the structure of successful organizations in different industries and different markets gives us insight into how to use capabilities, culture, and leadership as well as how to organize for a given strategy and specific type of innovation. At the same time, combining the results of observations and interviews, underlying research and current thinking, and experiments and previous knowledge has been proven to be productive when deciding on recommendations in practical situations. Section 5.11, "The Analysis and Recommendations Process," will further discuss strategies or recommendations as a part of the analysis process.

A common question about correlations is "What is a strong and what is a weak correlation?" One good rule of thumb is shown below:

Exactly -1: A perfect downhill (negative) linear relationship
−0.70: A strong downhill (negative) linear relationship
−0.50: A moderate downhill (negative) relationship
−0.30: A weak downhill (negative) linear relationship
0: No linear relationship
+0.30: A weak uphill (positive) linear relationship
+0.50: A moderate uphill (positive) relationship
+0.70: A strong uphill (positive) linear relationship
Exactly +1: A perfect uphill (positive) linear relationship

The most familiar measure of correlation between two quantities is the Pearson Product-Moment Correlation Coefficient or Pearson's Correlation Coefficient, commonly called simply the *correlation coefficient*. It is obtained by dividing the covariance of the two variables by the product of their standard deviations. The population correlation coefficient $\rho_{X,Y}$ between two random variables X and Y with expected values μ_X and μ_Y and standard deviations σ_X and σ_Y is defined as:

$$\rho_{X,Y} = \mathrm{corr}(X,Y) = \frac{\mathrm{cov}(X,Y)}{\sigma_X \sigma_Y} = \frac{E[(X-\mu_X)(Y-\mu_Y)]}{\sigma_X \sigma_Y}$$

where E is the expected value operator, *cov* denotes covariance, and *corr* is a widely used alternative notation for the correlation coefficient. The Pearson Correlation is defined only if both of the standard deviations are finite and nonzero.

Figure 25 illustrates several different data sets and their correlations using the Pearson formula.

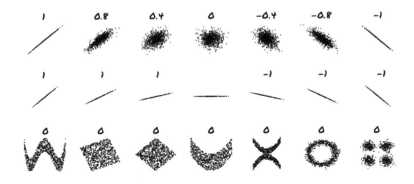

Figure 25. Several sets of (x, y) points, with the Pearson correlation coefficient of x and y for each set. Note that the correlation reflects the noisiness and direction of a linear relationship (top row), but not the slope of that relationship (middle), nor many aspects of nonlinear relationships (bottom). N.B.: the figure in the center has a slope of 0, but in that case, the correlation coefficient is undefined because the variance of Y is 0. (Source: Wikipedia, accessed May 27, 2017).

By adding a linear graph to the plot, it is easier to judge whether the correlation is strong or not, as shown in figure 26. Experience using InnoSurvey to measure and assess innovation characteristics has shown that a correlation between 0.4 and 0.5 is pretty indicative, while 0.3–0.4 is of interest. Below 0.3 is highly uncertain. However, if a strong relationship exists but is not linear, the correlation may be misleading, because in some cases, a strong curved relationship exists. That's why it's critical to examine the plot first.

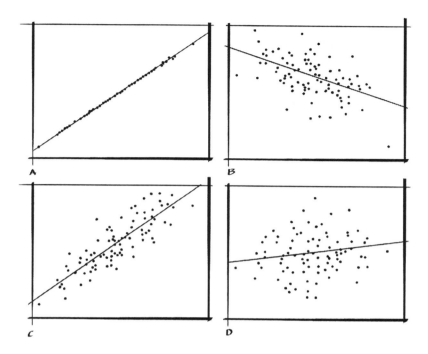

Figure 26. Diagrams with correlations of (a) +1.00, (b) -0.50, (c) +0.85, and (d) +0.15.

Capability	Corr.
Clear Vision	0.42
Goal Orientation	0.41
Innovation Priority	0.4
Innovation Measuring	0.39
Systematic Service Innovation	0.38
Idea Generation	0.37
System for Project Selections	0.37
Customers' Behavior Insights	0.36
Cross-Function	0.36
Evaluative	0.35

Table 6. Capability (from the sixteen aspects of the Wheel of Innovation) in correlation to Spiral Staircase leadership.

Capability	Corr.
Idea Diffusion	0.44
Innovation Priority	0.42
Systematic Service Innovation	0.41
Idea Generation	0.38
Cross-Function	0.38
Real Need Focus	0.36
General Involvement	0.34
DNA Focused	0.33
Format Development	0.33
Opportunistic	0.33

Table 7. Capability (from the sixteen aspects of the Wheel of Innovation) in correlation to Cauldron leadership.

5.10 Competence versus Capability

As discussed in section 3.9 and illustrated in table 5, both capabilities and competences are required to innovate in first, second, and third horizons in order to execute on an organization's strategic agenda and direction. Capabilities are seen as generic, while competence is found in more specialized fields. According to Assink (2006), the term *capabilities* emphasizes the key role of strategic management in appropriately adapting, integrating, and reconfiguring organizational skills, resources, and functional competencies to match the requirements of a changing environment.

Often, the term *knowledge* is used to describe what we specifically know, while *competence* is broader and includes cognitive ability (intelligence), motor skills, and artistic abilities. In this textbook, as in Innovation360 Framework for innovation, we use the term *capability* to mean the organizational ability of an enterprise to successfully undertake action that is intended to affect its long-term growth and both internal and external development. The term *competence* is used in its broad sense and means "knowledge that you are able to use on different levels: the collaborative network, organization, organizational unit, and an individual and personal level."

A capability can be the ability to set goals, while the related competence is the ability to follow a goal-setting framework to achieve the desired outcome. There are a number of checklists for goal-setting that can be learned and even understood, but gaining that competence does not mean the organization is ready to set goals. This particular case is, in fact, very common: managers and employees are sent to a course to learn to set goals that comprise the SMART Framework: Specific, Measurable, Attainable, Relevant, and Timebound, but the organization still fails to actually set goals, follow up on them, or—even more alarming—get any use out of it. Goal-setting is more than a competence to be learned or taught. It encompasses the values, mission, and vision that the whole organization is aligned to as well as a culture of taking responsibility and action for both the process and the outcome on both an individual and an organizational level. On the other hand, an organization ready to work in a specific, clear direction with responsibility and willingness to take action might be much better off learning how to structure goals and break them down into subgoals.

A more detailed example is how goals and innovation horizons are related. In the first horizon, goals are essential, and the Spiral Staircase leadership style (see section 3.5 on leadership styles), where goals are set and broken down into subgoals (basically one subgoal per increment), is useful. Any organization with the spiral leadership style and competence for SMART goal-setting is off to a pretty good start and will most likely have the capability of setting and working with goals. But in the second and third horizons, where a more explorative leadership style is preferable, goal-setting is harder. Even if everyone in the organization learned how to follow SMART goal-setting and developed goals that way, you would have to face the fact that an ambitious goal (as defined by SMART) might be very hard to break down into subgoals, simply because you don't know what steps to take. Extensive experimentation and learning are required to take the right steps, something that can hardly be put into a detailed project plan. Also, you will probably experience failure, most likely many times over. Leaders and employees risk losing faith and going back to ordinary incremental work and goals (first horizon) when resistance is high due to lack of vision and tangible proof. So even if you have an exploring leadership style and everyone is trained in goal-setting (a competence), goals around innovation will require collective growth in certain capabilities: being persistent; constantly experimenting, learning, and evaluating; moving in the direction of the overall goal; and not giving up in the face of temporary setbacks.

In Innovation360 Framework, sixty-six capabilities are identified as essential to innovation management, based on current thinking. These sixty-six capabilities are categorized into sixteen groups, which are shown as the axis of the Wheel of Innovation and are useful for measuring and assessing the innovation capabilities of an organization. Unlike capabilities, however, competencies are most likely infinite. For this reason, it's hard to predefine any structure for assessing competencies, so here assessments are typically adapted to the unique characteristics and needs of each organization.

5.11 The Analysis and Recommendation Process

Analyzing and generating recommendations can be based on a standard process like the one shown in figure 27. This is the recommended process for scoping the external and internal context and setting strategic direction, with short- and long-term goals for the organization. Sometimes, this process is already in place in an organization; other times, it needs to be structured by senior management or with outside expertise. (This is the theme of the fifth volume of this series.)

When analyzing external and internal context, the typical input includes the following:

- Strategic plans
- Business plans
- Brand manuals
- Marketing material
- Annual reports
- Profit and loss (P and L) statements
- Current balance sheet statement
- Offers, solutions, product samples
- Structure of service and product portfolios
- Marketing plans
- Competitor analyses
- Core process descriptions
- Organization chart
- Description of key personnel
- Description of core systems like Enterprise Resource Planning (ERP), product life-cycle systems, product document-management solutions, and so on

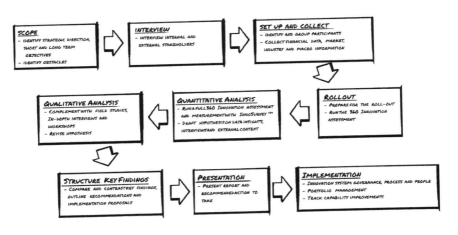

Figure 27: A basic innovation analysis and recommendation process (IAR).

5.11.1 Scoping, Interview, Setup, and Collection

In the process of scoping (framing a situation), identifying and working with stakeholders is the most crucial (and the hardest) part of assessing and measuring innovation strategy, leadership, culture, and capabilities and competences. From our long-time experience with assignments, we have learned the true importance of establishing common ground with purpose, language (concept), and a practical step-by-step process with frequent feedback to the stakeholders.

As it is when assessing and measuring innovation characteristics, grouping the stakeholders is a practical approach to managing the complexities of working with stakeholders, as you cannot involve and communicate to everyone at the same time and use the same language and message. One way to group stakeholders is to consider their level of power, legitimacy, and urgency. *Stakeholders with power* make decisions and make an impact on the organization; they are typically C-level executives but also some customers. A *stakeholder with legitimacy* is an authority, like an internal strategy manager, business developer, external journalist, regulatory authority, and so on. *Stakeholders with urgency* want results now and are typically internal project leaders, managers at all levels, and sometimes even customers or suppliers.

What we call *definite stakeholders* have all three—power, legitimacy, and urgency—and should be kept very close and involved in every step of the process. Stakeholders having two of the three components are called *expectant stakeholders* and should be kept informed on a regular basis and asked for feedback, although they are not as involved as definite stakeholders. Those with power, urgency, or legitimacy, the *latent stakeholders*, can be kept informed in a more formal and less frequent way. By dividing the stakeholders into these groups, it will be much easier for you to manage the amount of effort you put into each group, preventing the work from becoming impossibly demanding and time-consuming.

In section 5.3.2, "Assessments in Interviews," stakeholder interviews were described from a methodological point of view. With the groupings described above, the importance of conducting the interview based on the respondent's stakeholder group becomes apparent: if she is a definite stakeholder, for example, you should also spend some time talking about the assessment, but if she is a latent stakeholder, you would discuss the assessment more briefly. Whatever their stakeholder group, however, it is very important that all stakeholders involved in the process or the whole organization, and any external respondents be informed about the project, especially about the outcome and its implications. If everyone is not informed properly, this effort will be perceived as "just another project that is absolutely meaningless," creating a negative impact on the organization.

As we have discussed in earlier chapters, the qualitative data that is collected and codified in the scoping and interview stages of the process will be used together with quantitative data from the innovation measurement to form the basis for the complete innovation assessment.

After the interview and survey data are collected, make sure that all stakeholders receive communications about what the survey's purpose is and what the overall process looks like before sending out any survey. Most importantly, you need to create a common language by providing some background material and explain common connects used in the survey. The creation of a common language can be quite tricky, as the organization is most likely, at least partly, unconsciously incompetent

(Burch 1978) and therefore cannot be reached using a defined language and concepts about innovation that people do not yet understand.

Reaching out and creating common ground is essential. Establish purpose, language (concept), and a practical step-by-step process with frequent feedback to the stakeholders by defining a strategy for the stakeholders in all three groups: definite, expectant, and latent. Definite and expectant stakeholders are typically involved in workshops, interviews, and decision meetings, while latent stakeholders are simply kept informed. The challenge is to inform an organization that is unconsciously incompetent, which is a common problem in innovation management, as this is a new topic for many people. In assignments, we have used several techniques for this.

5.11.2 Rollout

There are many ways of rolling out the assessment and measurement of innovation. The decision should be based on the following points:

1. Organization-wide consciousness of present strategic direction and innovation as a concept
2. The complexity of the organization (how many employees, how many sites, how many languages, how many brands, etc.).

There are three common approaches (design implications of the survey will be discussed further in the appendix "Survey Design for Complex Assessments"), each of which is presented in the following sections.

5.11.2.1 Start Small and Establish an Innovation Task Force and Innovation Board

Often, it is preferable to start small. Innovation does not happen easily, and it requires substantial effort. If that were not the case, everybody would do it. Therefore, one recommended approach is to select a team, business unit, market, or brand to start with and apply the first iteration of the IAR process; then add new groups, one at a time (see figure 28 for an example from one of Innovation360's client cases). The implementation phase is as essential as the initial phase, as both phases establish common ground by internalizing common concepts such as hypothesis, experiment, risk, horizons, ideation, commercialization, and governing structures such as an innovation board and innovation task force. These concepts will be briefly discussed in section 5.11.5, "Implementation," in this volume, and in more detail in the third volume of this series.

In the beginning of the IAR, you establish purpose, create step-by-step plans, and introduce concepts; in the implementation phase, you actually internalize the concepts by practicing them. In the early phase of the IAR process, we recommend conducting workshops when implementing with a small team, while e-learning and study groups are alternative methods for large organizations (to be discussed in the coming chapters). When establishing concepts, regardless of setting or method, it is important to activate and stimulate the participants. Volume 4 of this series covers many different techniques (such as LEGO Serious Play) useful for internalizing concepts in the early phase and stimulating creativity and running experiments/prototyping (in the ideation work) in the later phase. For deeper understanding of learning and internalization, we recommend the study of *Experiential Learning* by Professor David A. Kolb (2014).

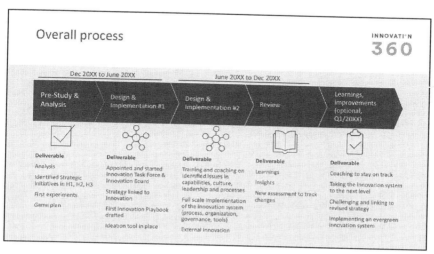

Figure 28: Slide from Innovation360 assignment with a first iteration followed by another iteration that enrolled the entire organization.

5.11.2.2 Champions and Study Groups

An alternative or complement to starting small is for just a part of the organization to roll out both the assessment and implementation of a full-scale innovation system. This topic will be covered in detail in the third volume of this series, *Working with Champions and/or Study Groups*.

The use of champions is a train-the-trainer concept where you appoint internal resources as trainers who guide the entire process, from measuring and assessing to design and implementation of a working innovation system within the organization. An alternative is to use study groups, where more self-organized groups are provided with material to study.

An innovation system consists of the following three major parts. This topic is covered in greater detail in the third volume of this book series.

1. **Innovation Process**: This process is divided into the *exploration* (ideation and project selection) and *execution* (development and commercialization) phases. The exploration phase is often executed by a special group within the organization (see below), while execution takes place within ordinary business activities in the form of projects, startups, or merger or acquisition of other organizations.

2. **Innovation Governance**: *Governance* is a term that describes how the innovation work is managed, including supporting and giving direction during the exploration phase; optimizing the execution phase with portfolio management of all projects; and prioritizing, allocating, and governing all assets driving the direction of the organization. We argue that the exploration phase is best run as one or several innovation task forces with a full-time chairperson and several learning and building personas from different parts of the organization creating links to the rest of the company. Moreover, we argue that the execution phase is best run within the existing business; if it is placed organizationally in separate units, prioritizations and allocation of assets should be centralized and governed by a designated innovation board with one chairperson. The chair of the innovation board should

be chosen based on his or her experience and ability to over-see difficult prioritization decisions with a neutral and analytical approach. Governance and the challenge of linking innovation activities to strategy and the organization as a whole is fully ex-plored in the fifth volume of this series.

3. **Innovation Organization**: The third component of an innovation system is its position within the organization and the people in-volved. The position (we call it "design choice") can be (1) as a central department, (2) in several collaborating satellites, or (3) fully integrated within the existing organizational chart. It can also be a combination of all three of these design choices. Each one has pros and cons. The centralized model is efficient, but innovation often occurs in other parts of the business or in the marketplace. Integrated innovation is easy to implement in first horizon strategies but very often hard or impossible to execute efficiently in second and third horizons, due to daily prioritiza-tions. Satellites are a mix of both and can be very efficient, but it can be hard to coordinate among them, as they normally are highly autonomous or allied with a specific part of the market or the organization.

Every organization must choose among these options based on its hori-zon strategy, industry and market, current level of innovation, and other unique internal and external factors. However, after many years working with companies of all sizes in many different markets, we found that in-novation systems are often better implemented in small steps, not as a formal, full-blown initiative from the first day.

5.11.2.3 E-Learning

An alternative or complement to champions and/or study groups is the use of e-Learning. E-Learning has many advantages: it can take place when, where, and however (like language, speed, reading, video, etc.) you like, but has the major disadvantage of lacking an oppor-tunity to discuss the material. We recommend overcoming this draw-back by integrating discussions, possibly connecting participants with trainers, and combining it with work in study groups. E-Learning can also be combined with online resources and competence tests, including recommendations and extra study material, interactive playbooks (methods and processes used by the organization), and ideation tools, providing a richer and more integrated approach than e-Learning alone.

5.11.3 The Quantitative and the Qualitative Analysis

The analysis is based on both external and internal information that can include both quantitative (like InnoSurvey data) and coded qualitative data (e.g., transcribed interviews, photos, and videos with notes). The analysis is the process where, based on the company's strategic direction, external context (opportunities and threats), and internal context (strengths and weaknesses), you figure out what's blocking forward motion and what could be done to amplify it.

As we've discussed in previous sections, understanding the data you have involves applying analytical techniques to find similarities and differences between groups by comparing their qualitative and quantitative data. Based on the resulting understanding of the data and the strategic direction, you can develop solutions that can achieve the following:

1. **Remove blockages** that are hindering or slowing down movement in the strategic direction. These are typically misalignments or lack of capabilities needed for a given leadership style or innovation strategy.
2. **Amplify the strategic direction**. One typical approach of this kind is to identify and initiate more innovation projects in the third horizon to support the second and first horizons. To do that, you can engage people in specific places in the organization who have the right leadership and capabilities to execute this approach (identified in your data analysis).

Recommendations should next be outlined based on the external and internal analysis, alignment, benchmarks, correlations, and the initial plans for removing blockages and amplifying the strategic direction of the organization. Typically, recommendations are based on one of three approaches such as the following:

- **Best Fit**, meaning they are based on how the current situation looks like and what's possible without any major changes. This approach is typically based on current conscious strategy, leadership, type of innovation, and the capabilities and competences that need to be strengthened.
- **Best in Class**, which are based on the best companies that have the same strategic intent you aim for. These recommendations focus on the changes needed in strategy, leadership, type of innovation, personas (the culture), capabilities, and competences.
- **Resource-Based View**, which is based on the company's current capabilities, personas, and competencies, focuses on what is realistically possible and how that can be aligned with the company's existing overall strategic direction by elaborating on innovation strategy, leadership, and type of innovation.

Each of these approaches is discussed in further detail in the following sections.

5.11.2.1 Best Fit

Best Fit is attractive to most organizations because organizations simply do not like change. Best Fit is a way of trying to improve on what is, rather than on what might be. Typically, you benchmark against known competitors and elaborate on what you already have and the direction you are already heading in. The advantage is that it will not take much time and most likely will not lead to any major internal challenges. The weakness, of course, is that it might be less useful for meeting the challenges emerging in your market. Our recommendation is to use this option only as the last alternative, as it often has very little impact and can actually hinder the organization from addressing the real challenges in a world that is changing faster than ever.

5.11.2.2 Best in Class

Best in Class is like Best Fit, but you compare yourself with the best organizations with a similar strategic direction, regardless of geography, customer base, or industry. This is a more ambitious approach than Best Fit and can often be accomplished incrementally and without major disruption to the company; however, it requires that your organization be open to change and that you learn from organizations outside your own industry.

5.11.2.3 Resource-Based View

The Resource-Based View (RBV) builds the competitive advantage of the company primarily through its application of a bundle of valuable tangible or intangible resources at the firm's disposal (Wernerfelt 1984, 172; 557–558; Penrose 1959). In order to transform a short-run competitive advantage into a sustained competitive advantage, these resources must be heterogeneous in nature and not be perfectly mobile (Peteraf 1993, 180). Effectively, this translates into valuable resources that are neither perfectly imitable nor substitutable without great effort.

In today's rapidly changing markets, critics have argued that it is not possible to maintain a competitive position solely by building on these resources (Barney, Wright, and Ketchen 2001, 117). However, in practice it is very useful—if you can use your resources (such as capabilities and specific competences unique to your organization) and keep on developing them. You can significantly increase your competitors' barriers to entry. On the other hand, it is a challenge and an ongoing expense to constantly build and use capabilities and competences as a means of maintaining and strengthening your position in the market.

5.11.4 Structuring the Presentation of Key Findings

As discussed in the previous section, recommendations should be based on the analysis of data and your design decisions about using the Best

Fit, Best in Class, or Resource-Based View approaches to implementing an innovation system. The presentation of these recommendations should summarize the key findings of this process and the logic used in reaching your conclusions. Moreover, link the recommendations to real observations with quotations from interviewees or survey respondents, pictures, and other qualitative material that strengthens your case.

5.11.4.1 Situation, Strengths, and Areas to Strengthen

Whether you present the recommendations verbally or in written form, it is important to communicate with impact. Start by describing the *situation* (external perspective; threats and opportunities), using the organization's own language and terminology (we call this *lingo*), and keeping your description brief and to the point. Continue with the *strengths,* which should be expressed as abilities and possibilities (internal perspective). Relate strengths to observations, interviews, and measurements, again using the organization's own lingo. It must be possible to verify or prove everything you say or write. The next topic is *areas to strengthen,* expressed as weaknesses (internal perspective), what is lacking, and what consequences we see. As with strengths, these areas are based on observations, interviews, and measurements. Again, you should be able to verify or prove anything expressed here—this is not the time for speculating. A common mistake is to give recommendations and solve problems at this stage. Do not attempt to do this; you will do that in the recommendations section. The purpose here is to reinforce what you have learned about pain points, market needs, and what the company lacks.

5.11.4.2 Recommendations

When presenting recommendations, use straightforward language expressed in the organization's own lingo. Be specific and relate each recommendation to the situation, strengths, and areas to strengthen that were just enumerated.

Formulate concrete value-generating actions that aim at reaching a defined strategic direction and related goals. If possible, also present breakthrough goals that will yield extraordinary outcomes. These recommended actions should have been verified during the planning process, in order to gain their acceptance by stakeholders through coaching, commenting, fully considered objections, and alignment exercises with groups and teams. A common mistake is to overlook the need for effective preparation, through consideration and appropriate handling of feedback and objections, so that the recommendations will get buy-in at an early stage in the process.

5.11.5 Implementation

Implementation is the subject of volumes 3 to 5 of this book series, but a brief overview will be given here. Basically, implementation is designing the organization to support innovation, design plans for needed changes, implement changes step-by-step, and secure the result of each step in terms of both expected organizational behavior and business results.

Typically, implementation is undertaken either in several iterations or in one large project that uses cascading techniques like study groups and champions, as discussed in section 5.11.2.2.

Implementation should be based on the recommendations and linked to clear outcomes that are either of the following:

1. **Behavioral change** based on strategy, processes, leadership, personas/cultures, capabilities, and/or competences. Behavioral changes are typically tracked by running new follow-up surveys using a system like InnoSurvey that measures, assesses, and tracks the improvement of innovation characteristics and competences.

2. **Business results** like profit, growth, and improved, radically changed, or completed new types of innovations (e.g., processes, products, business models, and services). Business results are typically linked to key performance indicators (KPIs) and monthly or quarterly follow-up at a managerial level.

As discussed in chapter 5.11.2.2, there are three parts of an innovation system such as the following:

1. **Innovation Process**: Divided into *exploration* (ideation and project selection) and *execution* (development and commercialization).
2. **Innovation Governance**: How to manage the innovation work.
3. **Innovation Organization**: The people involved and the position within the organization. Design choices include: (1) a central department, (2) several collaborating satellites, or (3) full integration within the existing organizational chart.

To implement the designed innovation system, it is imperative to link it to the behavioral changes needed and the prerequisites for that change. (What's feasible and what's less feasible?) As you as a reader might have guessed, we have lived through this, and we feel passionate about it! We have seen consultants and internal planners airily wave their hands about as if to say, "I've given you the plan, so now it's up to you to magically implement it!" In our experience, those are the plans that sit on people's bookcases and credenzas and are forgotten within six months. It's not fair to managers to expect them to think at this meta level when they're being bitten to death by ducks every day. You need to be present, to coach, and to help. In our opinion and approach, it should be based on facts and insights, and that's why you measure and assess before starting to implement innovation-management systems.

5.12 Study Questions

Go to https://innovation360.com/assessment/ and complete the free version of InnoSurvey for your (or your client's) organization, based on your perception. When you have completed the survey, read the analysis of the report and ask yourself the following questions:

5-1) Is the described *strategy* consistent with my perceived strategy of the organization?

5-2) Is the described *leadership* consistent with my perceived leadership of the organization?

5-3) Is the described *type of innovation* consistent with my perceived type of innovation of the organization?

5-4) Are the described *capabilities* consistent with my perceived capabilities (the "footprint" in the report) of the organization?

5-5) Is the described *innovation process* consistent with my perceived innovation process of the organization?

5-6) Are the described *personas* consistent with my perceived personas of the organization?

Then ask yourself the following questions:

5-7) How do you think externals, like partners, would answer these questions, and why?

5-8) How do you think managers would answer these questions, and would they answer the same as each other or not? Why?

5-9) How do you think employees would answer these questions, and would they answer the same as each other or not? Why?

5-10) Where do you think people would answer most differently, and why?

5-11) Why is it important to do a 360 analysis (i.e., measuring and assessing groups of external and internal respondents) to be able to give useful recommendations?

CHAPTER 6

CEN STANDARD AND ISO STANDARD FOR INNOVATION ASSESSMENT

There have been several standardization efforts, both national and international, on innovation management/capability assessment going on all over the world for the last several years, but the two most important initiatives are the already-published European CEN standard (the CEN/TS 16555 Part 7: Innovation Management Assessment) and the ongoing work within the technical committee ISO/TC 279 on the new ISO standard for innovation-management systems (the ISO 50500, on innovation-management assessment, that is expected to be published sometime in late 2018, according to their current plan.

As Innovation360 group is participating in the ongoing work of ISO/TC 279, especially the Working Group 4 (WG4) on Innovation Management Assessment; we are both contributing to and getting early insights into the standard as it evolves toward finalization. Based on these contributions and insights, our perception is that although the CEN/TS 16555 has been around for a few years, and that ISO standard is still in the midst of its development, they will have a lot in common in the end, and will be recognized as reinforcing rather than contradicting each other. This convergence is very good for the global innovation community, as it will stipulate a credible and common ground for best practice innovation-management assessment in the world!

In this chapter of the book, we will focus on describing the general outlines and common grounds of the two standards and the general outline of the Innovation360 group's process for innovation assessment, the Innovation Assessment with Recommendations (IAR) process.

We will then finish by discussing what we believe is the basis for the standards compliance of the IAR.

Note that both the CEN/TS 16555 standard (formally still a technical specification under development) and the upcoming ISO 50500 standard will be so-called *guiding standards*, as opposed to certification standards. Hence, there will not be any third-party audits for certification, meaning that compliance here will have the semantics of *in line with the guidance* rather than *fulfilling the formal requirements.*

6.1 The CEN and ISO Standards Common Ground for Best-Practice Innovation Management Assessment

Both the CEN and the ISO standards will define the context, scope, and purpose and role of innovation-management assessment (IMA) in similar ways, and they are both targeted as a means to assess, analyze, and continuously improve an innovation-management system (IMS). Hence, the IMS is the assessment object.

Both standards will be based on the same notion of recurring assessments for continuous improvement (performance) of both the innovation-management system and the IMA process itself. To track progress, both standards will probably use the same four-level maturity model for innovation-management systems put forward in the CEN standard (i.e., a model that defines four levels of maturity, from Level 1: "Ad-Hoc" to Level 4: "Innovation as part of the organizational DNA." See the CEN/TS 16555 Part 7 for the full specification of this model).

Both the CEN and the ISO standards will define a set of different approaches for an IMA, spanning from simple manual checklists and interviews to largely automated survey and analysis processes, including benchmarking assessments based on a common innovation database for comparison.

Both standards define the outcome of an IMA as a gap analysis for the strengths and weaknesses of the IMS as a starting point for its continuous improvement.

Both standards will also be based on a combination of quantitative assessment in the form of surveys (largely subject to automation) and qualitative assessment, including external analysis and interviews (typically, manual work). Hence, an IMA will typically be conducted through a combination of automated surveys, tool-supported analysis (such as benchmarking) and manual interviews and external analysis (such as PESTLED analysis).

We will now look through the main elements of the two IMA standards and then discuss how our IAR process, its underlying Innovation Framework (chapter 4) and the InnoSurvey assessment tool (chapter 5) comply with these standards.

6.2 The CEN/TS 16555—Part 7: Innovation-Management Assessment

The CEN/TS 16555 defines three types of assessment approaches: checklist assessment, maturity assessment, and benchmarking assessment.

The checklist assessment uses a seven-degree scale to capture the respondents' perception of a number of predefined capability/performance factors in a checklist questionnaire going in incremental steps from *very low* to *very high*.

The maturity assessment uses the four-degree maturity model as illustrated here:

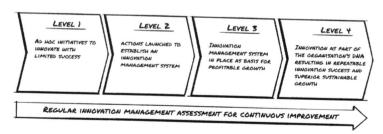

Figure 29: The four-level innovation-management maturity model as defined in the CEN/TS 16555-Part 7: Innovation-Management Assessment.

The *benchmarking assessment model* uses a spider-diagram technique to compare the data of an assessment with a selection of benchmark data. The benchmarking assessment is based on the fact that there exists a relevant common database on innovation management for comparison.

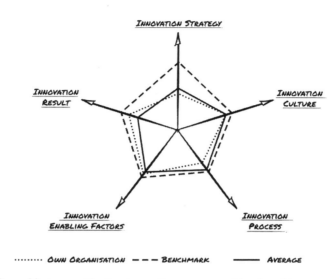

Figure 30: An example of an innovation-management benchmarking assessment as defined in the CEN/TS 16555-Part 7: Innovation-Management Assessment.

The assessment process itself is described as a process with three phases, in accordance with the following graph from the CEN/TS 16555: Part 7 document.

Figure 31: Phases of an innovation-management assessment as defined in the CEN/TS 16555-Part 7: Innovation-Management Assessment.

Bottom line: according to the CEN 16555 standard, an IMA is conducted as a combination of interviews, surveys, and desk research, all regarding both quantitative measures and qualitative measures, and the methods used will be self-assessment (e.g., the individual perceptions of survey respondents), expert analysis, and third-party validation.

The results of an IMA are referred to as a gap between the actual result of the assessment compared to the target results for the innovation-management system (IMS) being assessed. Based on the assessment, the organization should then define, communicate, and execute an action plan for the improvement of the assessed IMS. This should be a recurring process also for the continuous improvement of the assessed IMS.

Apart from the main document, there are also two annexes to the CEN/TS 16555 Part 7 document that provides more details and some useful information. These are *Annexe A (Informative)*: "Comparison of innovation-management assessment methods and finding the right tools" and the normative *Annexe B (Normative)*: "Deliverables and expected impact from innovation-management assessment."

6.3 The ISO 50502 Son Innovation Management Assessment[8]

As of June 2017, the upcoming ISO 50502 standard on innovation-management assessment (IMA) is still being developed within WG4. These efforts will be complemented by a guiding document defining the principles of the IMA called Principles for Innovation Management Assessment (PIMA).

The PIMA document will provide seven principles to facilitate the design and implementation of the IMA, as defined in the standard, and is intended to give an overall orientation to the users implementing the IMA in their organizations. The seven principles are given as follows:

1. Add value to the organization.
2. Challenge the organization's strategy and objectives.
3. Motivate and mobilize for organizational development.

---

8 This is a working name, as this work is still ongoing.

4. Be timely and focused on the future.
5. Allow for context and promote the adoption of best practices.
6. Be flexible and holistic.
7. Be an effective and reliable process.

The key elements of the draft IMA standard will be defined based on the PIMA principles. Hence, it will assume the best practice of recurring assessments and continuous realization of the benefits of its outcomes. It will also assume that the IMA process itself will be continuously improved.

The following early sketch illustrates the sections of the IMA working draft currently discussed in WG4.

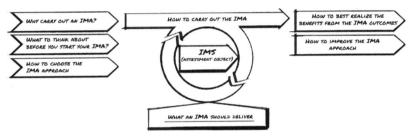

Figure 32: An early sketch visualizing the innovation-management assessment process and the assessed "object," the innovation-management system itself.

The IMA standard will start defining the why, what, and how of the IMA, guiding the users to clearly define the organization's reasons for doing the IMA, how to plan and set up the IMA in the best possible way, and how to choose an appropriate approach to conducting the IMA. This may eventually have a different structure from the CEN/TS 16555 standards, but it will most likely be very close semantically to the definitions in the CEN standard.

The assessment itself will probably be more elaborate than in the CEN standard and define guidelines for choosing different approaches, external and/or internal respondents, different representation/presentation formats (such as five- to seven-degree psychometric scales), color abacus scales (or other normalized scales where data is presented as histograms), maturity grades, and/or spider diagrams (*footprints*).

It will probably also give guidance on suitable company metadata and other relevant metadata for benchmarking assessment using an innovation database.

The IMA is then expected to be carried out by applying the approach of choice, in practice using a combination of manual and automated processes and tools very much like the definition in the CEN/TS 16555 standard. Here too, of course, the outcomes (the gaps between actual and target factors of the IMS) are then subject to realization by defining, communicating, and executing an action plan to realize the proposed (implementation) projects as well as an appropriate time for the next assessment, and so on, as a means to continuously improving the performance of the assessed IMS.

6.4 Innovation360 Group's Process for Innovation Assessment with Recommendations (IAR)

Innovation360 Group bases its assessment technology, the InnoSurvey platform, on a formalized, research-based Innovation Framework, as defined by Mr. Magnus Penker in his studies leading up to his 2008 MBA from Henley Business School.

The Innovation Framework (as described in detail in chapter 4) is a unique synthesis of research on current thinking and generally accepted innovation best practices. It is centered around a core of sixty-six innovation capabilities but is also formally interrelated with other why, what, and how questions, putting the assessed innovation capabilities in a formalized context of innovation strategy, type of innovation strategy, type of innovation, innovation leadership styles, and innovation personas.

Most of these factors are mentioned in the two assessment standards as relevant aspects of an IMA, but they are not formalized in any way beyond that.

When we perform an IMA at Innovation360 Group, we do it in accordance with our process called Innovation Assessment with Recommendations, or IAR (chapter 5.11).

The IAR is illustrated and described in more detail in chapter 5.11, but we will repeat it here for the sake of the following compliance discussion.

The phases of the IAR process are illustrated in the figure 33:

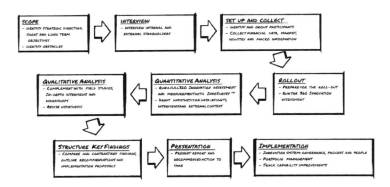

Figure 33: The Innovation360 process of innovation assessment with recommendations.

The IAR process is conducted as a combination of manual work and automated work, using our assessment tool InnoSurvey, which provides automation and tool support for both the survey part and the analysis part. The survey part consists of a ninety-three-question questionnaire with a possibility to set up a number of respondents representing different external and internal roles (our definition of a 360 approach) and manage the entire data-collection process. The analysis part, the capability analyzer, supports the quantitative analysis of data both by benchmarking and correlation analysis, for capability pattern recognition using our Wheel of Innovation (our own framework-specific application of a spider diagram) and our large innovation database that today holds data from more than one thousand companies all over the world.

The quantitative analysis also provides a type of *maturity level* indicator, the InnovationIQ. Our InnovationIQ index spans from zero to one hundred and is an indicator to track innovation-management system performance improvement over time through recurring assessments. Although there is no formal relationship between InnovationIQ and the CEN/ISO IMS maturity levels, they are both intended to provide a tool for tracking continuous improvement of the IMS. Hence, one can think of the mapping between InnovationIQ and the four maturity levels as: 0–25 ≈ maturity level 1; 25–50 ≈ maturity level 2; 50–75 ≈ maturity level 3; and 75–100 ≈ maturity level 4.

As presented in chapter 4, the quantitative analysis part of the IAR is also complemented with qualitative analysis and interviews to finally arrive at key findings and implementation recommendations for the improvement of the assessed innovation-management system.

6.5 IAR Standards Compliance Discussion

From studying the CEN/TS 16555 and based on our insights on the upcoming ISO 50502 standards, in accordance with sections 1.2 and 1.3, we believe that the IAR process provides a complete solution for benchmarking assessment that in practice can be regarded as a super-set to the CEN/ISO standards.

We also believe our thinking behind the IAR (as described in chapters 4 and 5) is in full harmony with the Principles on Innovation Management Assessment (the PIMA document) of the upcoming ISO standard.

The IAR process is based on using our Innovation Framework and the InnoSurvey tool covering all the concepts defined and presented in the standards in a more formally encoded way. It also allows us to do metadata-based, precise filtering for benchmarking, including advanced filtering such as applying *xor* logic. InnoSurvey also provides support for benchmark analysis through pattern recognition or correlation analysis. This is a very powerful assessment-analysis technique, not mentioned at all in the CEN/TS 16555 standard. In theory, much of this can be done manually, but InnoSurvey allows us to do this more efficiently and with very high data precision, something we refer to as either *evidence-based recommendations* or *data-driven recommendations*.

The only model presented in the standards that is not currently implemented in the IAR process is the four-degree innovation maturity model. But as we presented in chapter 1.4, we do believe that there is a reasonably good mapping between our InnovationIQ-ratings and the four levels of the IMS maturity model.

So, for the automated parts of the IAR (quantitative analysis), based on the above reasoning, we believe that the IAR complies fully with the published CEN/TS 16555 and will comply fully with the upcoming ISO 50502 standard (when published). For the manual parts of the IAR (quantitative analysis), one can always adopt one's ways of working for full compliance as required.

A final conclusion on the compliance issue is that the IAR approach is most likely not only compliant with the CEN/ISO standards, but it also takes the best practices of innovation-management assessment a good step further beyond them.

CHAPTER 7

APPENDIX: SURVEY DESIGN FOR COMPLEX ASSESSMENTS

A number of questions typically arise when a complex organization is about to be measured and assessed. Two of the most frequent questions concern the optimum number of groups to divide an organization into and the optimum number of survey respondents from each of these groups. As you might expect, the answers depend on the complexity of the organization being assessed. In a non-complex organization, where one or two groups are being measured and assessed, each unit can have between ten and a hundred respondents. Surprisingly, having more than this adds little value; it might be done for political reasons or so that everybody can be included, but in practice, it yields very little extra information. But when you are assessing a complex organization with multiple group structures, you might have to measure and assess six units, ten units, or more. In that case, based on our experience, anywhere between seven and twenty-five respondents per unit is sufficient, although more may be surveyed for political reasons. However, always study the organizational structure before defining a group or determining how many units to assess, as this will help support an effective analysis later.

Another question that often arises when complex organizations are being assessed and measured is whether there is a need for sponsors. In our practical experience, we have found that there does need to be a sponsor in complex organizations, an executive who can motivate staff and defend the measurement and assessment findings. Typically, the CFO, business-development manager, or a project manager are good candidates—they tend to have intimate knowledge about the direction the company is heading in, both financially and strategically. It is a good idea to let this sponsor take the first survey and show the results to help him or her get a first feeling of an assessment as well as how the organization's capabilities stand up against industry benchmarks.

Communication is essential during this assessment and measurement phase, as it is often hard to get the message through. Start by setting up a communication plan with fixed dates for deadlines. Make sure that all definite stakeholders (and eventually, expectant stakeholders as well) get an introductory e-mail before the rest of the organization does, making them aware of the upcoming survey, its purpose, and its importance. This communication should clearly state that the survey is for the betterment of the organization and is supported by senior management—otherwise stakeholders might respond with political opposition, out of fear or misunderstanding.

However, just informing via e-mail will not be enough. Communication must be planned and done in all relevant channels such as intranet, newsletter, posters as well as information meetings or kickoffs, and through other established channels. Make sure to describe the channels, the message, and the target group to each and when to reach them (before, during, and after assessment) in the communication plan.

As part of the communication plan, you will also need to send reminders about completing the survey, especially in complex and large organizations. The initial survey e-mail is not enough; everyone is busy and can miss it or simply forget about it. A reminder plan that specifies exactly when to send a reminder (for example, halfway between the start date and deadline) is important. This simple task can be invaluable, as it increases the participation rate, thus improving the quality of the assessment.

CHAPTER 8

REFERENCE LIST

Amabile, Teresa. M. 1998. "How to Kill Creativity." *Harvard Business Review* 76 (5): 76–87.

Assink, M. 2006. "Inhibitors of Disruptive Innovation Capability: A Conceptual Model." *European Journal of Innovation Management* 9 (2): 215–253.

Barney J. B., M. Wright, and D. J. Ketchen Jr. 2001. "The Resource-Based View of the Firm: Ten Years after 1991." *Journal of Management* 27 (6): 625–641.

Benton, H. H., ed. 1974. *Encyclopaedia Britannica.* 15th ed. London: Encyclopedia Britannica, Inc.

Boudreau, K. J., and K. R. Lakhani. 2009. "How to Manage Outside Innovation." *MIT Sloan Management Review,* 50 (4): 69–77.

Brown, T., and R. Martin. 2015. "Design for Action." *Harvard Business Review* 46 (9): 56–64.

Burch, N. 1978. "Porter, or Ambivalence." *Screen* 19 (4): 91–105.

Brinkinshaw, J., C. Bouquet, and J. Barsoux. 2011. "The 5 Myths of Innovation." *MIT Sloan Management Review* 52 (2): 43–50.

Casadesus-Masanell, R., and F. Zhu. 2010. "Business Model Innovation and Competitive Imitation: The Case of Sponsor-Based Business Models." *John Wiley & Sons, Ltd* 34 (4): 464–482.

Catmull, E. 2008. "How Pixar Fosters Collective Creativity." *Harvard Business Review* 86 (9): 41–50.

Chesbrough, H. 2011. "Bringing Open Innovation to Services." *MIT Sloan Management Review* 52 (2): 85–90.

Coyne, K. P., P. G. Clifford, and R. Dye. 2007. "Breakthrough Thinking from Inside the Box." *Harvard Business Review* 85 (12): 70–78.

Danneels, E. 2002. "The Dynamics of Product Innovation and Firm Competences." *Strategic Management Journal* 23: 1095–1121.

D'Aveni, R. A. 1995. "Coping with Hypercompetition: Utilizing the New 7S's Framework." *Academy of Management Executive* 9 (3): 45–60.

Day, G. S. 2007. "Is It Real? Can We Win? Is It Worth Doing? Managing Risk and Reward in an Innovation Portfolio." *Harvard Business Review* 85 (12): 110–120.

D'Aveni, R. A., B. G. Dagnino, and K. G. Smith. 2010. "The Age of Temporary Advantage." *Strategic Management Journal* 31: 1371–1385.

Drucker, P. F. 1998. "The Discipline of Innovation." *Harvard Business Review* 76 (6): 149–157.

International Federation for Information Processing. 1998. *The FRISCO Report—A Framework of Information System Concepts*, edited by Falkenberg, E. D., W. Hesse, P. Lindgren, B. E. Nilsson, J. L. Han Oei, C. Roland, R. K. Stamper, F. J. M. Van Assche, A. A. Verrijn-Stuart, and K. Voss), accessed June 29, http://www.mathematik.uni-marburg.de/~hesse/papers/fri-full.pdf.

Flynn, B. B., S. J. Wu, and S. Melnyk. 2010. "Operational Capabilities—Hidden in Plain View." *Business Horizons* 53: 247–256.

Gallo, C. 2011. *The Innovation Secrets of Steve Jobs—Insanely Different Principles for Breakthrough Success*. New York: McGraw-Hill.

Govindarajan, V., and C. Trimble. 2005. "Organizational DNA for Strategic Innovation." *Califonia Management Review* 47 (3): 47–76.

Grunert, K. G., and C. Ellegaard. 1992. "The Concept of Key Success Factors: Theory and Method." *Market based Process and Product Innovation in the Food Sector*-MAPP, working paper, no. 4 (ISSN 0907 2101).

Hamel, G. 2006. "The Why, What, and How of Management Innovation." *Harvard Business Review* 84 (2): 72–84.

Hansen, M. T., and J. Birkinshaw. 2007. "The Innovation Value Chain." *Harvard Business Review* 85 (6): 121–130.

Haq, K., and A. K. Sen. 2011. "Product Innovation by Small and Medium-Sized Firms through Outsourcing and Collaboration." *International Journal of Management and Marketing Research* 4 (1): 61–73.

Huston, L., and N. Sakkab. 2006. "Connect and Develop: Inside Procter & Gamble's New Model for Innovation." *Harvard Business Review* 84 (3): 58–66.

Jaruzelski, B., and K. Dehoff. 2010. *The Global Innovation 1000: How the Top Innovators Keep Winning.* New York: Booz & Company, Inc.

Jaruzelski, B., V. Staack, and B. Goehle. 2014. "Proven Paths to Innovation Success." *Strategy+Business* 77 (winter 2014).

Johnson, M. W., C. M. Christensen, and H. Kagermann. 2008. "Reinventing Your Business Model." *Harvard Business Review* 86 (12): 51–59.

Kelly, T., and J. Littman. 2005. *The Ten Faces of Innovation.* New York: Doubleday.

Kim, W. C., and R. Mauborgne. 2005. "Value Innovation: A Leap into the Blue Ocean." *Journal of Business Strategy* 26 (4): 22–28.

Kim, W. C., and R. Mauborgne. 1997. "Value Innovation: The Strategic Logic of High Growth." *Harvard Business Review* 75 (4): 103–112.

Kolb, A. David. 2014. *Experiential Learning: Experience as the Source of Learning and Development,* 2nd ed. New Jersey: Pearson FT Press.

Le, T. 2008. "A Dual Economy Model of Endogenous Growth with R&D and Market Structure." *Journal of Evolutionary Economics* 18 (3–4): 349–366.

Leonard, D., and S. Straus. 1997. "Putting Your Company's Whole Brain to Work." *Harvard Business Review* 75 (4): 28–38.

Loewe, P., P. Williamson, and R. C. Wood. 2001. "Five Styles of Strategy Innovation and How to Use Them." *European Management Journal* 19 (2): 115–125.

McKim, R. 1973. *Experience in Visual Thinking.* Monterey, CA: Brooks/Cole Publishing Co.

McKinsey & Company. 2009. "Enduring Ideas: The Three Horizons of Growth," accessed June 1, http://www.mckinsey.com/business-functions/strategy-and-corporate-finance/our-insights/enduring-ideas-the-three-horizons-of-growth.

Sawhney, M., R. C. Wolcott, and I. Arroniz. 2006. "The 12 Ways for Companies to Innovate," *MIT Sloan Management Review* 47 (3): 75–81.

Nambisan, S., and M. Sawhney. 2007. "A Buyer's Guide to the Innovation Bazaar." *Harvard Business Review* 85 (6): 109–116.

Ohr, R. C., and K. McFarthing. 2013. "Managing Innovation Portfolios: Strategic Portfolio Management," accessed June 1, http://www.innovationmanagement.se/2013/09/16/managing-innovation-portfolios-strategic-portfolio-management/.

O'Reilly, C., and Tushman, M. 2004. "The Ambidextrous Organization." *Harvard Business Review* 82 (4): 74–81.

Osterwalder, A., and Y. Pigneur. 2010. *Business Model Generation: A Handbook for Visionaries, Game Changers, and Challengers.* New York: John Wiley and Sons.

Penker, M., and H. E. Eriksson. 1997. *UML Toolkit.* New York: John Wiley and Sons.

Penker, M., and H. E. Eriksson. 2000. *Business Modeling with UML. Business Patterns at Work.* New York: John Wiley and Sons.

Penker, M., et al. 2003. *UML 2 Toolkit.* New York: John Wiley and Sons.

Penker, M. 2011a. "A Communication and PR Model for International Management Consultants." LinkedIn Slideshare, accessed June 29, https://www.slideshare.net/magnuspenker/a-communication-and-pr-model-for-international-management-consultants-2011-official-version.

Penker, M. 2011b. "A Structure and Model for How to Build Intellectual Capital in a Management Consulting Company." LinkedIn Slideshare, accessed June 29, https://www.slideshare.net/magnuspenker/a-structure-and-model-for-how-to-build-ic-in-a-management-consulting-company-2011-official-version.

Penker, M. 2011c. "Innovation Key Success Factors for SMEs Acting on Niche Markets." LinkedIn Slideshare, accessed June 29, https://www.slideshare.net/magnuspenker/innovation-key-success-factors-for-sme-acting-on-nisch-markets.

Penker, M. 2016. *"Organizing for Simultaneous Innovation Capability—Key Findings from +1,000 Companies."* Presented at the Drucker Forum, Vienna, November 2016.

Penrose, E. T. 1959. *The Theory of the Growth of the Firm.* New York: John Wiley and Sons.

Peteraf, M. A. 1993. "The Cornerstones of Competitive Advantage: A Resource-Based View." *Strategic Management Journal* 14 (3): 179–191.

Porter, M. E. 1985. *Competitive Advantage: Creating and Sustaining Superior Performance*. New York: Free Press. Reprinted in abridged form in De Wit, R., and R. Meyer. 2004. *Strategy: Process, Content, Context: An International Perspective*. 3rd ed., 258–267. London: Thomson.

Porter, M. E. 1980. *Competitive Strategy: Techniques for Analyzing Industries and Competition*. New York: Free Press.

Porter, M. E. 1990. *The Competitive Advantages of Nations*. New York: Free Press.

Porter, M. E. 1996. "What Is Strategy?" *Harvard Business Review* 74 (6): 61–78.

Quelin, B. 2000. "Core Competencies, R&D Management, and Partnerships." *European Management Journal* 18 (5): 476–487.

Ramaswan, S. N., M. Bhargava, and R. Srivastava. 2004. *Market-Based Assets and Capabilities, Business Processes, and Financial Performance*. Cambridge: Marketing Science Institute.

Ries, E. 2011. *The Lean Startup: How Today's Entrepreneurs Use Continuous Innovation to Create Radically Successful Businesses*. New York: Crown Publishing.

Rigby, D. K., K. Gruver, and J. Allen. 2009. "Innovation in Turbulent Times." *Harvard Business Review* 87 (6): 79–86.

Rigby, D., and C. Zook. 2002. "Open-Market Innovation." *Harvard Business Review* 80 (10): 80–89.

Scott, A., D. Duncan, and P. Siren. 2015. "Zombie Projects: How to Find Them and Kill Them." *Harvard Business Review* 93, accessed June 29, https://hbr.org/2015/03/zombie-projects-how-to-find-them-and-kill-them.

Shrieves, R. E. 1978. "Market Structure and Innovation: A New Perspective." *The Journal of Industrial Economics* XXVI (4): 329–347.

Simon, H. 1969. *The Sciences of the Artificial*. Cambridge: MIT Press.

Teece, D. J. 2010. "Business Models, Business Strategy, and Innovation." *Long Range Planning* 43: 172–194.

Tovstiga, G., and D. W. Birchall. 2005. *Capabilities for Strategic Advantage—Leading Through Technological Innovation*. Basingstoke: Palgrave Macmillan.

Trott, P. 2008. *Innovation Management and New Product Development*. 4th ed. Essex: Pearson Education Limited.

Webster's. 1992. *New Webster's Dictionary and Thesaurus of the English Language*. School, home and office ed. Lexicon Publications.

Wernerfelt, B. 1984. "The Resource-Based View of the Firm." *Strategic Management Journal* 52: 171–180.

About the Authors

Magnus Penker

Magnus Penker is an internationally renowned thought leader on innovation, digitization, and business transformation. He has spoken at prestigious global forums and events including the Global Peter Drucker Forum, top-ranked international business schools, a variety of associations, and some of the world's largest companies.

He has been honored with two *Business Worldwide Magazine* awards for his achievements, the "Most Innovative CEO Sweden 2016" and "Growth Strategy CEO of the Year Sweden 2016" awards. Additionally, he has launched ten startups and has acquired, turned around, and sold more than thirty European SMEs.

Through his best-selling American books on digitization and IT engineering, and his more than twenty years of experience as a management consultant and business leader, Mr. Penker inspires leaders to find a new way of thinking and organizing to stay on top.

For the past eight years, he has used his practical and theoretical insights to develop InnoSurvey, a leading methodology and global innovation database that is used for business analysis and support to companies, business leaders, and scientists around the world. Today, Mr. Penker is the CEO and founder of the Innovation360 Group, headquartered in Stockholm, Sweden, and New York in the United States.

Mr. Penker is driven by the recognition that in these turbulent times, we must understand our core strengths and determine how we can use those capabilities and competencies to create advantages in a globalized market with endless possibilities. The global map is being redrawn at speeds never before seen, and historically low interest rates are attracting capital to global digital-risk projects that will further strengthen this movement.

Mr. Penker has a BSc in Computer Science (CTH, Sweden) and an MBA from the Henley Business School, England.

Peter Junermark

Peter Junermark is an acclaimed trainer who has brought his skills to some of the world's most recognizable brands. As a leader of Innovation360 workshops, Peter specializes in bringing disruptive technology and breakthrough projects to life. He is the senior software architect and lead developer with primary responsibility for the platform supporting the tools of the Innovation360 Group.

Before joining the Innovation360 Group, Peter was cofounder and a senior manager at Open Training Sweden's Gothenburg office. During his long-term consultancy at the Volvo Information Technology headquarters, Peter built learning-management and competence-management systems.

As one of the initial contributors to the Innovation360 Framework, Peter brings to this series of volumes a deep understanding of the theoretical foundations of his work. Peter's training background and logically ordered thinking proved to be invaluable in explaining the most complex relationships in plain language with examples that are easy to visualize.

Peter holds a master of science in computer engineering from Chalmers University of Technology in Gothenburg, Sweden. His latest projects involve the investigation of cutting-edge AI that expand on agile methodologies and establish an easily sharable set of coding principles.

Sten Jacobson

Sten Jacobson has successfully managed more than two hundred management-consulting assignments, during which he challenged board members, executive teams, and managers to keep pressing for more creative yet profitable business models, often with sustainability at the core of the differentiation.

He is a master at the practical applications of Blue Ocean strategy creation, which is designed to unearth one-of-a-kind, data-derived pockets of uncontested markets. He shows companies how to redraw industry boundaries in such a way that it essentially makes competition irrelevant.

Sten is the leading instructor for the accreditation of Innovation360's global cadre of licensed practitioners. He has been instrumental in spreading the InnoSurvey results and methodologies out to every continent. He has engaged within workgroups at the ongoing international standardization work (ISO) on innovation-management systems and innovation-management assessment. Among Sten's most in-demand skills are his expertise in executive-team mentoring, power conceptualization/visualization, seismic disruption, and the applications of advanced tech within professional services. His speaking engagements for C-level execs and international associations also frequently center on his work in value-proposition design, business-process mapping, and digital transformation.

He brings to this series a wider perspective on strategic execution of Innovation360 principles, translating the mechanics of innovation into management standards and practices that can be put into effect the moment the innovation team is assembled.

Sten holds a master of science in electronic engineering from the Royal Institute of Technology (KTH) in Stockholm, Sweden. He also holds higher-management education from the Stockholm School of Economics (SSE) in Stockholm.

INDEX

Made in the USA
Columbia, SC
25 August 2017